CHINESE IMMIGRATION

Marissa K. Lingen

THE CHANGING
Face of North America:
IMMIGRATION SINCE 1965

CHINESE IMMIGRATION

Marissa K. Lingen

MASON CREST PUBLISHERS
PHILADELPHIA

Produced by OTTN Publishing, Stockton, New Jersey

Mason Crest Publishers
370 Reed Road
Broomall, PA 19008
www.masoncrest.com

First printing

1 3 5 7 9 8 6 4 2

Library of Congress Cataloging-in-Publication Data

Lingen, Marissa.
  Chinese immigration / Marissa K. Lingen.
    p. cm. — (The changing face of North America)
Summary: An overview of immigration from China to the United States and Canada since the 1960s, when
immigration laws were changed to permit greater numbers of people to enter these countries.
Includes bibliographical references and index.
  ISBN 1-59084-694-X
1. Chinese Americans—History—20th century—Juvenile literature. 2. Chinese—Canada—History—20th
century—Juvenile literature. 3. Immigrants—United States—History—20th century—Juvenile literature.
4. Immigrants—Canada—History—20th century—Juvenile literature. 5. China—Emigration and immigration—
History—20th century—Juvenile literature. 6. United States—Emigration and immigration—History—20th
century—Juvenile literature. 7. Canada—Emigration and immigration—History—20th century—Juvenile literature. [1. Chinese Americans—History—20th century. 2. Chinese—Canada—History—20th century.
3. Immigrants—United States—History—20th century. 4. Immigrants—Canada—History—20th century.
5. China—Emigration and immigration—History—20th century. 6. United States—Emigration and immigration—
History—20th century. 7. Canada—Emigration and immigration—History—20th century.] I. Title. II. Series.
  E184.C5L597 2004
  304.8'73051--dc22
                                                          2003016369

THE **CHANGING**
Face of North America:
IMMIGRATION SINCE 1965

CONTENTS

INTRODUCTION

THE CHANGING FACE OF AMERICA

By Senator Edward M. Kennedy

America is proud of its heritage and history as a nation of immigrants, and my own family is an example. All eight of my great-grandparents were immigrants who left Ireland a century and a half ago, when that land was devastated by the massive famine caused by the potato blight. When I was a young boy, my grandfather used to take me down to the docks in Boston and regale me with stories about the Great Famine and the waves of Irish immigrants who came to America seeking a better life. He talked of how the Irish left their marks in Boston and across the nation, enduring many hardships and harsh discrimination, but also building the railroads, digging the canals, settling the West, and filling the factories of a growing America. According to one well-known saying of the time, "under every railroad tie, an Irishman is buried."

America was the promised land for them, as it has been for so many other immigrants who have found shelter, hope, opportunity, and freedom. Immigrants have always been an indispensable part of our nation. They have contributed immensely to our communities, created new jobs and whole new industries, served in our armed forces, and helped make America the continuing land of promise that it is today.

The inspiring poem by Emma Lazarus, inscribed on the pedestal of the Statue of Liberty in New York Harbor, is America's welcome to all immigrants:

Give me your tired, your poor,
Your huddled masses yearning to breathe free,
The wretched refuse of your teeming shore,
Send these, the homeless, tempest-tossed, to me:
I lift my lamp beside the golden door.

The period since September 11, 2001, has been particularly challenging for immigrants. Since the horrifying terrorist attacks, there has been a resurgence of anti-immigrant attitudes and behavior. We all agree that our borders must be safe and secure. Yet, at the same time, we must safeguard the entry of the millions of persons who come to the United States legally each year as immigrants, visitors, scholars, students, and workers. The "golden door" must stay open. We must recognize that immigration is not the problem—terrorism is. We must identify and isolate the terrorists, and not isolate America.

One of my most important responsibilities in the Senate is the preservation of basic rights and basic fairness in the application of our immigration laws, so that new generations of immigrants in our own time and for all time will have the same opportunity that my great-grandparents had when they arrived in America.

Immigration is beneficial for the United States and for countries throughout the world. It is no coincidence that two hundred years ago, our nations' founders chose *E Pluribus Unum*—"out of many, one"—as America's motto. These words, chosen by Benjamin Franklin, John Adams, and Thomas Jefferson, refer to the ideal that separate colonies can be transformed into one united nation. Today, this ideal has come to apply to individuals as well. Our diversity is our strength. We are a nation of immigrants, and we always will be.

FOREWORD

THE CHANGING FACE OF THE UNITED STATES

Marian L. Smith, historian
U.S. Immigration and Naturalization Service

Americans commonly assume that immigration today is very different than immigration of the past. The immigrants themselves appear to be unlike immigrants of earlier eras. Their language, their dress, their food, and their ways seem strange. At times people fear too many of these new immigrants will destroy the America they know. But has anything really changed? Do new immigrants have any different effect on America than old immigrants a century ago? Is the American fear of too much immigration a new development? Do immigrants really change America more than America changes the immigrants? The very subject of immigration raises many questions.

In the United States, immigration is more than a chapter in a history book. It is a continuous thread that links the present moment to the first settlers on North American shores. From the first colonists' arrival until today, immigrants have been met by Americans who both welcomed and feared them. Immigrant contributions were always welcome—on the farm, in the fields, and in the factories. Welcoming the poor, the persecuted, and the "huddled masses" became an American principle. Beginning with the original Pilgrims' flight from religious persecution in the 1600s, through the Irish migration to escape starvation in the 1800s, to the relocation of Central Americans seeking refuge from civil wars in the 1980s and 1990s, the United States has considered itself a haven for the destitute and the oppressed.

But there was also concern that immigrants would not adopt American ways, habits, or language. Too many immigrants might overwhelm America. If so, the dream of the Founding Fathers for United States government and society would be destroyed. For this reason, throughout American history some have argued that limiting or ending immigration is our patriotic duty. Benjamin Franklin feared there were so many German immigrants in Pennsylvania the Colonial Legislature would begin speaking German. "Progressive" leaders of the early 1900s feared that immigrants who could not read and understand the English language were not only exploited by "big business," but also served as the foundation for "machine politics" that undermined the U.S. Constitution. This theme continues today, usually voiced by those who bear no malice toward immigrants but who want to preserve American ideals.

Have immigrants changed? In colonial days, when most colonists were of English descent, they considered Germans, Swiss, and French immigrants as different. They were not "one of us" because they spoke a different language. Generations later, Americans of German or French descent viewed Polish, Italian, and Russian immigrants as strange. They were not "like us" because they had a different religion, or because they did not come from a tradition of constitutional government. Recently, Americans of Polish or Italian descent have seen Nicaraguan, Pakistani, or Vietnamese immigrants as too different to be included. It has long been said of American immigration that the latest ones to arrive usually want to close the door behind them.

It is important to remember that fear of individual immigrant groups seldom lasted, and always lessened. Benjamin Franklin's anxiety over German immigrants disappeared after those immigrants' sons and daughters helped the nation gain independence in the Revolutionary War. The Irish of the mid-1800s were among the most hated immigrants, but today we all wear green on St. Patrick's Day. While a century ago it was feared that Italian and other Catholic immigrants would vote as directed by the Pope, today that controversy is only a vague memory. Unfortunately, some ethnic groups continue their efforts to earn acceptance. The African

Americans' struggle continues, and some Asian Americans, whose families have been in America for generations, are the victims of current anti-immigrant sentiment.

Time changes both immigrants and America. Each wave of new immigrants, with their strange language and habits, eventually grows old and passes away. Their American-born children speak English. The immigrants' grandchildren are completely American. The strange foods of their ancestors—spaghetti, baklava, hummus, or tofu—become common in any American restaurant or grocery store. Much of what the immigrants brought to these shores is lost, principally their language. And what is gained becomes as American as St. Patrick's Day, Hanukkah, or Cinco de Mayo, and we forget that it was once something foreign.

Recent immigrants are all around us. They come from every corner of the earth to join in the American Dream. They will continue to help make the American Dream a reality, just as all the immigrants who came before them have done.

FOREWORD

THE CHANGING FACE OF CANADA

Peter A. Hammerschmidt
First Secretary, Permanent Mission of Canada to the United Nations

Throughout Canada's history, immigration has shaped and defined the very character of Canadian society. The migration of peoples from every part of the world into Canada has profoundly changed the way we look, speak, eat, and live. Through close and distant relatives who left their lands in search of a better life, all Canadians have links to immigrant pasts. We are a nation built by and of immigrants.

Two parallel forces have shaped the history of Canadian immigration. The enormous diversity of Canada's immigrant population is the most obvious. In the beginning came the enterprising settlers of the "New World," the French and English colonists. Soon after came the Scottish, Irish, and Northern and Central European farmers of the 1700s and 1800s. As the country expanded westward during the mid-1800s, migrant workers began arriving from China, Japan, and other Asian countries. And the turbulent twentieth century brought an even greater variety of immigrants to Canada, from the Caribbean, Africa, India, and Southeast Asia.

So while English- and French-Canadians are the largest ethnic groups in the country today, neither group alone represents a majority of the population. A large and vibrant multicultural mix makes up the rest, particularly in Canada's major cities. Toronto, Vancouver, and Montreal alone are home to people from over 200 ethnic groups!

Less obvious but equally important in the evolution of Canadian immigration has been hope. The promise of a better life lured Europeans and Americans seeking cheap (sometimes even free) farmland. Thousands of Scots and Irish arrived to escape grinding poverty and starvation. Others came for freedom, to escape religious and political persecution. Canada has long been a haven to the world's dispossessed and disenfranchised—Dutch and German farmers cast out for their religious beliefs, black slaves fleeing the United States, and political refugees of despotic regimes in Europe, Africa, Asia, and South America.

The two forces of diversity and hope, so central to Canada's past, also shaped the modern era of Canadian immigration. Following the Second World War, Canada drew heavily on these influences to forge trailblazing immigration initiatives.

The catalyst for change was the adoption of the Canadian Bill of Rights in 1960. Recognizing its growing diversity and Canadians' changing attitudes towards racism, the government passed a federal statute barring discrimination on the grounds of race, national origin, color, religion, or sex. Effectively rejecting the discriminatory elements in Canadian immigration policy, the Bill of Rights forced the introduction of a new policy in 1962. The focus of immigration abruptly switched from national origin to the individual's potential contribution to Canadian society. The door to Canada was now open to every corner of the world.

Welcoming those seeking new hopes in a new land has also been a feature of Canadian immigration in the modern era. The focus on economic immigration has increased along with Canada's steadily growing economy, but political immigration has also been encouraged. Since 1945, Canada has admitted tens of thousands of displaced persons, including Jewish Holocaust survivors, victims of Soviet crackdowns in Hungary and Czechoslovakia, and refugees from political upheaval in Uganda, Chile, and Vietnam.

Prior to 1978, however, these political refugees were admitted as an exception to normal immigration procedures. That year, Canada revamped its refugee policy with a new Immigration Act that explicitly affirmed Canada's commitment to the resettlement of refugees from oppression. Today, the admission of refugees remains a central part of Canadian immigration law and regulations.

Amendments to economic and political immigration policy continued during the 1980s and 1990s, refining further the bold steps taken during the modern era. Together, these initiatives have turned Canada into one of the world's few truly multicultural states.

Unlike the process of assimilation into a "melting pot" of cultures, immigrants to Canada are more likely to retain their cultural identity, beliefs, and practices. This is the source of some of Canada's greatest strengths as a society. And as a truly multicultural nation, diversity is not seen as a threat to Canadian identity. Quite the contrary—diversity *is* Canadian identity.

1 BEYOND GOLD MOUNTAIN

J ust 100 years ago, the Chinese population in the United States was small, and most Chinese Americans lived in major cities. They had left their home in East Asia to earn their fortune in the land that many referred to as "Gold Mountain."

By the beginning of the 21st century, first- and second-generation Chinese immigrants had become part of every city in the United States and Canada. Today they are workers in every industry, and most city neighborhoods have at least one Chinese family. Chinese enclaves are also prevalent in the traditional Chinatowns of major U.S. cities as well as in the more-Americanized suburban neighborhoods.

Chinese immigrants today are more likely to dream of making their fortune with high-technology silicon rather than the gold that some of their ancestors discovered. Regardless, North America is still a land of great opportunity for many newcomers.

The People of China

Encompassing much of eastern Asia, China is the fourth-largest country in the world. Although it is slightly smaller than the United States, it contains the world's largest population of 1.3 billion people. Officially known as the People's Republic of China, the country has 22 provinces, although the ruling government considers the island of Taiwan to be its

◀ The Great Wall of China, an ancient fortification that extends 1,500 miles (2,400 kilometers), is the country's most recognized landmark. Chinese immigrants have been leaving their home country for Canada and the United States since the 19th century; after living through periods of discrimination in both countries, the Chinese have become the largest immigrant group to Canada and the fourth largest to the United States.

23rd province. China also contains five autonomous (or self-governing) regions, dominated by minority ethnic groups that have been allowed limited power (such as Tibet), and two special administrative regions—Hong Kong and Macao—which have their own executive, legislative, and judicial powers. The country's capital, Beijing, is one of four special municipalities.

People unfamiliar with China sometimes think it is an ethnically homogeneous country, but in fact it is home to many different minority groups. In addition to the more than 90 percent of the Chinese populace who belong to the Han ethnic group,

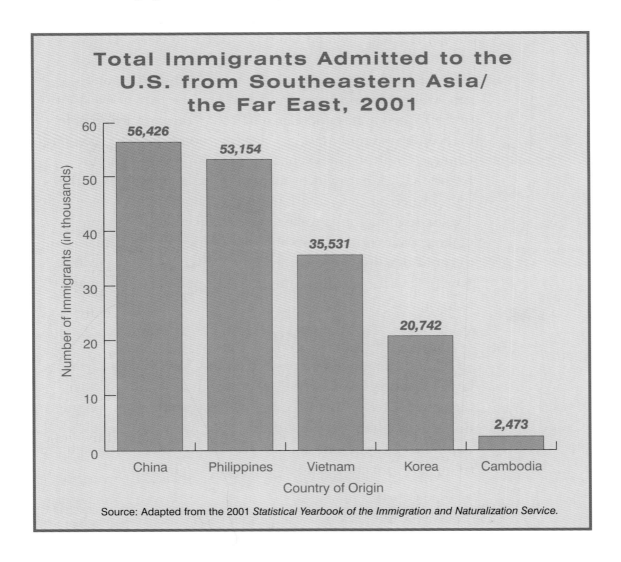

Total Immigrants Admitted to the U.S. from Southeastern Asia/ the Far East, 2001

Source: Adapted from the 2001 *Statistical Yearbook of the Immigration and Naturalization Service.*

Acupuncture and the Chinese Influence on Western Medicine

China has the world's oldest living civilization, and some of its practices date back for many centuries. Acupuncture is one traditional Chinese discipline in the field of health and medicine that has increasingly been adopted by non-Chinese people.

Acupuncture is an ancient Chinese method of relieving pain and treating disease by inserting needles into specific areas of the body. Acupuncturists believe that pain and disease are caused by imbalances in the body between the two principal forces of nature known as *yin* and *yang*. Ailments occur when one force is stronger than the other; acupuncture is a method of equalizing the balance between these forces.

Practiced throughout Asia and Europe, acupuncture has gained acceptance with many people in the United States and Canada. Some members of the medical profession find that acupuncture is useful as a helpful, additional treatment to other Western medicines; others find it to be an acceptable alternative in its own right. Most U.S. states and Canadian provinces regulate and grant licenses to establishments that offer acupuncture.

there are 55 other groups recognized by the government, the largest of which include the Zhuang, Manchu, Hui, Miao, Uygur, Yi, Mongolian, Tibetan, Buyi, and Korean. Some of these minorities are concentrated in one region—the majority of Tibetans live in Tibet, for example—but others are dispersed throughout the whole country.

More than 70 percent of the Chinese speak Mandarin (Putonghua), the official language of China that originated in the north. The rest of the population speaks a number of Chinese dialects, which include Yue (Cantonese), Wu (Shanghaiese), Minbei (Fuzhou), Minnan (Hokkien-Taiwanese), Xiang, Gan, and Hakka.

As is common with many Communist countries throughout history, China is officially atheist and claims no national religion. However, an estimated 100 million Chinese practice

Buddhism and Taoism, and a very small percentage of the population follows Islam, Christianity, and other religions.

One of the Largest Immigrant Groups

In 2001 Chinese people made up the fourth-largest ethnic group immigrating to the United States, behind Mexico, India, and the Philippines. During that same year, Chinese immigrants comprised the largest ethnic group entering Canada. On average, about 30,000 Chinese immigrate to Canada each year.

According to the 2000 U.S. Census, approximately 2.7 mil-

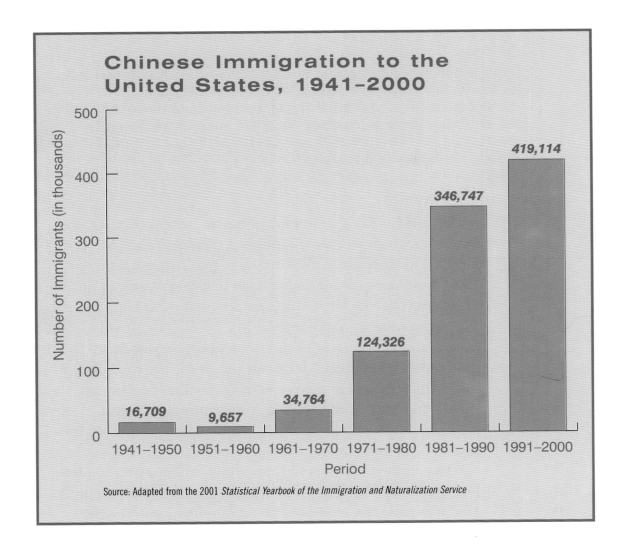

Chinese Immigration to the United States, 1941–2000

Source: Adapted from the 2001 *Statistical Yearbook of the Immigration and Naturalization Service*

lion Chinese now live in the United States, making them the largest Asian group in the United States. The Chinese make up more than 20 percent of the 11.9 million people of Asian origin. The number of people of Chinese ancestry living in Canada has also increased significantly during the latter half of the 20th century. In the 1996 and 2001 Canadian census reports, speakers of Chinese dialects ranked behind only French- and English-speakers. The 2001 census also indicated that 332,825 people, or about 1 percent of the 30 million living in Canada, were from China.

Growing Migration Numbers

The path from China to North America has often been harrowing, causing many difficulties for those looking to immigrate. Many have died or have had to return to their homeland before they made it to their destination. Some of the obstacles have been placed by the homeland government, some by destination countries, and some by the choppy seas along the travel route. On the other hand, some Chinese immigrants have enjoyed a comfortable and modern jet trip to Toronto, Los Angeles, or New York.

But no matter how they have reached the continent, Chinese immigrants have continued to come to North America in large numbers. During the 1990s, legal immigrants from China averaged 42,000 a year, or 115 a day. Undocumented immigrants have added to that total, though their population numbers are hard to determine. What is certain is that Chinese Americans will make up an increasing part of American culture in the decades to come, contributing to nearly all aspects of American life.

2

THE ERA OF REVOLUTION

During the 19th and early 20th centuries, China endured decades of economic hardship and the intervention of foreign powers, in particular Japan, which continually sought to gain control of Chinese land. The second half of the 20th century has been marked by revolution and internal friction.

The 1930s was a period of political chaos from which arose two opposing Chinese leaders: Chiang Kai-Shek of the Nationalist Party, which had ruled a united China since 1916, and Mao Zedong of the Communist Party. Chiang Kai-Shek was an anti-Communist who had a military background and had worked hard at consolidating and modernizing the Chinese government. However, Mao Zedong showed great faith in the peasants of the countryside and won their favor, calling on them to form his "peasants' and workers' army."

During the 1930s Japan seized Chinese territories in the north and east, while the Nationalists fought the Communists in a civil war. In 1941 the Nationalist government entered World War II, and fought against Japan until the end of the war in August 1945. The war years caused great hardships for Chinese citizens, as the Japanese occupation was brutal and far-reaching. In the "good" years, the ordinary Chinese people lived under grinding poverty; in bad years, many starved to death.

The Second World War considerably undermined Chiang

◀ One of the most influential leaders of the 20th century, Mao Zedong (1893–1976) was founder of the People's Republic of China, established in 1949. As the leader of the Communist Revolution in the 1940s and chairman of the Communist Party, Mao was a pivotal force behind the political and economic transformation of China.

Kai-Shek's Nationalist government, and it lost to Mao Zedong's forces during the Communist Revolution of the 1940s. On October 1, 1949, the People's Republic of China was formally established. Three months later, Chiang Kai-Shek and his close advisors fled to the island of Taiwan, which was traditionally a province of China. There the Nationalist Party set up a government in exile, and for decades, this tiny island was recognized by many other world nations, including the United States, as the site of China's legitimate government. The governments of Taiwan and the People's Republic of China have each claimed to be the true government of the Chinese people, forcing other countries to choose which of the two to recognize.

In front of a poster of Chairman Mao Zedong, a group of Chinese schoolchildren read from the "Little Red Book," the nickname for the famous book of quotations by Mao. Public readings like this one were common during the Cultural Revolution (1966–76), a national movement launched to make Chinese society more uniformly Communist.

Under the Rule of Mao Zedong

Mao Zedong and his inner circle of advisors decided to give themselves time to establish their newly chosen form of government. During a five-year planned transition to a socialist system (1953–57), Chairman Mao called upon "a hundred flowers to bloom," and "a hundred schools of thought to contend." Everyone was encouraged to criticize the government for the purpose of improving it. But the hundred flowers soon withered: government officials used the criticisms to identify opponents of the government and punish them. Dissidents were forced to work as beasts of burden in the fields, pulling carts like horses or oxen. Many were denied medical care; some killed themselves.

Many Chinese found Mao a charismatic and popular figure, and his image was promoted around China. His portraits and statuettes were offered for sale in all of the provinces, and he had several collections of poetry and proverbs published. The most famous was *Quotations from Chairman Mao Zedong*, also referred to as the "Little Red Book." Mao wanted to improve China's economy through various agricultural and industrial programs that together constituted the "Great Leap Forward." He demanded that no one resist the plan—not the peasants, intellectuals, or even his fellow party members. But the ideas of the Great Leap Forward didn't work out as planned. For example, the Communist leadership believed that building small steelmaking furnaces in every village would eliminate the need for large factories, but this plan failed, and by 1958 production had plummeted.

The Great Leap Forward soon proved a failure in many other ways. Persons committed to Communist ideals were delegated to run farms and factories even if they lacked ability or experience. An even more pressing problem was the poorly devised policies that led to mismanagement of China's agriculture and industry. Lacking the information that comes from the free pricing of goods and the absence of market incentives that encourage productivity and innovation, the Chinese economy, like those of other Communist countries, suffered. And so did China's people: during the early 1960s, at least 20 million people died of starvation over the course of three years. Rather than blaming themselves for their intrusive policies and poor planning, Communist Party leaders blamed the ordinary peasants for the famine, accusing them of hoarding grain in their homes.

The Cultural Revolution (1966–76)

In 1966 Chairman Mao Zedong instituted sweeping cultural changes. China's Cultural Revolution was intended to destroy all "reactionary" or "elitist" elements of Chinese culture that had existed before the revolution of the 1940s. To form a perfect Communist state and supposedly fix all of China's social ills, the "enemies of the people" had to be rooted out. Many students and other young people joined the Red Guards—paramilitary groups responsible for carrying out Mao's doctrines as they saw fit.

Men and women of the Red Guards recite Communist Party propaganda at a rally in Tiananmen Square in 1966. Primarily composed of Chinese youth, the Red Guards were loyal paramilitary groups that used extreme methods to enforce party policy.

Controversy over Tibet

Home to the world's tallest peak, Mount Everest, the mountainous region of Tibet has been under the control of China for over a half-century. One of the least developed regions in China, Tibet has no railroad and one of its counties even has no roads at all. The region is particularly hard hit during times of famine.

Before the Chinese entered Tibet, it was run by a religious government of Buddhist spiritual leaders whose two central figures were the Panchen Lama and the Dalai Lama. In 1951 Tibet surrendered its authority to the Chinese, although it kept its right to regional self-government.

For decades the Dalai Lama, whom his followers consider the reincarnation of the Buddha of Compassion, has maintained a Tibetan government in exile, and through nonviolent means has pressured the People's Republic of China to give Tibet the same status as that granted to Hong Kong (a special administrative region with its own executive, legislative, and judicial powers). Meanwhile, the Chinese government has suppressed Tibetan Buddhism by closing or destroying monasteries, and arresting or persecuting monks, nuns, and other separatists. Tibetan separatism has gained support in the West from those who argue that China is abusing Tibetans' basic human rights and their right to religious freedom. Although China's rule over Tibet is controversial, the region remains firmly a part of the People's Republic of China.

Chinese people had long been taught that they had "four big rights": speaking freely, airing one's views fully, holding debates, and writing large-character posters. Chinese youth in the Red Guards took these four big rights to great extremes in criticizing Mao's enemies. The guards were encouraged to hate the intelligentsia and to use any means necessary, including torture, to identify anti-revolutionaries. For example, some students forced their teachers to kneel on broken glass while they screamed at them for hours.

Even Deng Xiaoping, who was then secretary-general of the Communist Party, and who would eventually succeed Mao as chairman, was not immune from the purges. He was removed from office and sent to a remote prison camp. No one was in a high enough position to be protected, nor was anyone lowly enough to escape notice. Anyone who angered one of the Red Guards could be set upon in the middle of the night. Members of the Red Guards were even known to turn on each other.

By the end of the 1960s China was in shambles. More famines occurred, with even the most basic food staples becoming unavailable to hungry peasants. As a result of Mao's policies, many thousands starved to death. Many others tried to flee China, even though it was illegal to do so. Some of them found sanctuary in the United States and Canada.

Debate continues today in China and beyond as to how much Mao knew about the starvation and violence taking place among the Chinese people during the Cultural Revolution. Some scholars maintain that Mao was fully informed about the famines and the use of labor camps. Others claim that he got his information from lower party officials, who concealed the truth in order to appear supportive of his policies and receive promotions.

Mao was also influenced by the so-called Gang of Four, which included his wife Jiang Qing and three of her followers—Wang Hongwen, Yao Wenyuan, and Zhang Chunqiao. Through their involvement in propaganda and the national arts, these four influential leaders made grabs for power while attempting to bring every aspect of Chinese life under Communist control.

In 1972, beginning with the visit of U.S. President Richard Nixon to China, American-Chinese relations improved. But although the U.S. government and its people began to develop positive feelings toward China, little changed for the Chinese people under the Communist regime. In her book *Asian American Experiences in the United States*, author Joann Faung Jean Lee interviewed Chinese immigrant Kenny Lai about why he chose to leave China in the early 1970s. He explained:

> [F]or those of us who had no connections, we could plan on spending the rest of our lives there [on a farm commune]. I thought that as long as I didn't marry, maybe I could withstand it. I could stand spending the next forty to fifty years on the

Jiang Qing (1914–91), wife of Mao Zedong, stands trial in 1981. Jiang was a member of the infamous Gang of Four that was tried and convicted of treason during the administration of Deng Xiaoping. Many people believed that the gang's imprisonment was proof that the Cultural Revolution had ended.

commune. But I was thinking when I got married, my children would be forced to stay there, and my children's children. So future generations would be forced to be farmers. So there was no way out. If they wouldn't let me leave, the only thing to do was escape.

Almost all Chinese immigrants to the United States, Canada, or other countries during the early 1970s believed that by leaving China they had escaped a horrible fate not only for them but for their children and grandchildren.

In 1976, Chairman Mao died. Upon his death, many Chinese people felt a sense of shock and loss that is hard for most Westerners to understand. Although Mao had been responsible for policies that killed millions of Chinese people, he had also helped develop the national identity of Communist China. Over the years his sayings had become a part of common speech. And while not everyone liked his methods, many believed that his rule effectively guided the country. The period after his death was marked by profound uncertainty for most people living in China.

Deng Xiaoping and the "Four Modernizations"

Shortly after Mao's death, Hua Guofeng became Communist Party chairman. He had already become China's premier following the death of Premier Zhou Enlai in January 1976. Determined that the Chinese government not remain under the thumb of the Gang of Four, Hua had the gang members arrested. Their imprisonment meant the end of their power in China, as well as the end of the Cultural Revolution. Each of the four leaders was sentenced to death, though the sentences were later reduced to life imprisonment.

By the early 1980s Hua had been replaced by Deng Xiaoping, who had strong ideas about how to improve the economic situation of the Chinese people. In the early 1960s, when Premier Zhou had called for the modernization of four sectors—agriculture, industry, defense, and science and technology—the Cultural Revolution had swept away his efforts. In 1975, Zhou tried again to institute reforms with the help of Deng, at that time recently "rehabilitated" and returned to political life after being forced into a rural prison camp. Finally, after the arrest of the Gang of Four, Deng was able to incorporate the plans for the "Four Modernizations" into official state policy.

Deng Xiaoping was in some ways a more personable leader than Mao. He was less revered but more liked. He was even affectionately addressed by his first name in some student parades, and his statements of daily philosophy were popular, but by no means as treasured as the sayings of Chairman Mao. While political and religious freedoms continued to be suppressed under Chairman Deng's rule, he was a more practical Chinese Communist, and his policies did not lead the people into crises like those of earlier years did.

China's One-Child Policy

In front of a memorial adorned with flower wreaths, two Chinese men mourn the death of Mao Zedong, September 1976. Although at the time many Westerners were relieved that Mao's reign of power had come to an end, the majority of Chinese people felt a great loss following the death of the revered leader.

One of the major differences between Mao and Deng's policies stemmed from their different attitudes toward China's population. During the early years of Mao's administration, the Chinese government favored high population growth. Despite the country's many widespread famines, Mao and his ministers believed that large families were necessary in order to provide as many workers as possible for the Chinese economy. Moreover, in traditional peasant societies large families served a practical function, as their members would provide for each other and assist elders who would someday retire.

The policy of encouraging China's citizens to have large families remained in place for a few years after Mao's death. But as Deng became confident in his leadership, his government began to evaluate how it could feed its millions—and determined that it could not. As a result the Chinese government decided to

U.S. President Jimmy Carter (right) and Premier Deng Xiaoping speak at a press conference in Washington, D.C., January 1979. Later that year China and the United States established full diplomatic relations, one of many steps toward reconciliation that first began with President Richard Nixon's 1972 visit to China.

attempt to solve the crisis by persuading its citizens to have smaller families.

The plan remained in place during the 1970s, and in 1980 was codified into what is known as the "one-child policy." According to the new standards, Chinese couples were allowed to have only one child, and the Chinese government took severe measures to make sure this policy was followed. In many provinces, women were forced to undergo late-term abortions and sterilizations. All pregnant women had to have *shengyu zheng*, or birthing licenses, with them when they went to the hospitals to deliver their babies.

Some Chinese people believe that the one-child policy is good for the country because it will help keep the burgeoning population under control and thus minimize hunger, poverty, and other social ills. Others believe that it is wrong for the government to dictate what people do within their own families, and they complain that government intervention is coercive and at times violent. Many human rights groups agree with these critics, and have denounced the one-child policy and its restrictions, citing them as significant human rights violations.

The right of privacy has been almost entirely lacking in Communist China. In the towns, village elders keep track of any infractions committed by residents. In the cities, each person is monitored by a street committee, which keeps track of sanitation, traffic, birth control, and the general behavior of the citizens. This repressive system of scrutiny and prosecution has been a primary reason why Chinese people have decided to leave their homeland.

Many Chinese families today have only one child, in accordance with a government policy introduced during the early 1980s. The one-child law, controversial among many international human rights groups, was designed to limit China's population size.

Zhang Boli's Escape from China

Growing up in China during the 1960s, a decade of misery, terror, and famine, Zhang Boli was well acquainted with death. "Almost every day, people died of starvation in the surrounding villages," he states in his memoir *Escape from China: The Long Journey From Tiananmen to Freedom*, published in 2002. But he was horrified to learn later that people living in other regions had experienced far worse conditions. "[W]hen I became a reporter, I learned that the area where I lived was among those with the smallest number of deaths caused by famine," he recalled. His outrage at the conditions of the Chinese peasants during his childhood led him to actively protest against the Communist government.

As a leader in the Tiananmen Square Democracy Movement, 26-year-old Zhang, along with fellow students Guo Haifeng and Bai Meng, led the marchers into the square. The students believed that the government would be caught off-guard by the protest and would not initiate violence against them, a belief Zhang later realized was naive.

After the massacre on June 4, thousands of students fled the square. Twenty-one of them soon learned that they, including Zhang, had been placed on the Chinese government's "Most Wanted" list. After spending two years as a fugitive in rural northeastern China, Zhang was eventually smuggled into Hong Kong. From there he made his way to Los Angeles, California, where as a recent convert to Christianity, he has worked as a minister and public speaker.

Tiananmen Square Democracy Movement

The human rights crisis in Communist China has lasted for decades. Many Chinese people who came of age during the Cultural Revolution remain wary of speaking out about their rights, fearing that such criticisms would once again bring the Red Guards to their door. It wasn't surprising, then, that the first major protest movement against the Communist government drew most of its leaders from a segment of the population that was too young to remember the Cultural Revolution in detail.

Young dissidents, mostly university students in Beijing, began a large-scale protest in the city's Tiananmen Square on April 15, 1989. Their demands were many: They wanted to be able to choose their leaders, rather than having them selected from among veteran party leaders, by the veteran party leaders themselves. They sought the freedom to organize and the right to express their beliefs. They also called for an end to government corruption, an improvement of the educational system, and leniency for previous victims of political persecution.

Tiananmen Square, located in the Chinese capital of Beijing, was the site of the June 1989 massacre of hundreds of student protesters. The demonstrators had made demands for more democratic freedoms, which the communist leadership perceived as a threat to the government's power.

The Communist government interpreted the students' demands and the growing democracy movement as a threat to its own power. On June 4 government soldiers and tanks entered the square, killing hundreds and injuring thousands of the demonstrators. Thousands more fled in fear for their lives. Some were captured and imprisoned, while others made it out of the country, later settling in North America, Australia, Europe, or other parts of Asia.

The Tiananmen Square incident shocked the Chinese people, making them even more distrustful of their government. Many decided to leave the country by whatever means possible, and emigration from China—both legal and illegal—increased in numbers that would have been unheard of in the 1960s or even the 1980s.

A Change in Economic Policy

After Deng Xiaoping died in 1997, Jiang Zemin became the leader of the Communist Party in China. He was the first supreme leader in almost 100 years who did not owe his rise to power to military intervention or control. Although Jiang still

Chinese president Jiang Zemin meets with President George W. Bush at a news conference in October 2002. Elected in 1997, Jiang ushered in economic reforms as president that have moved China's economy closer toward a free-market system.

had close ties to the People's Army, he also understood how to achieve his goals through political means rather than exclusively through military force.

Jiang continued to follow the economic policies initiated under Deng. In the early 1990s, after realizing that it could not succeed economically under a strict Communist system, the government made changes. It allowed for the privatization of some of the farming communes and then of some businesses and factories. The Communist Party characterizes this economic system as Chinese-style Communism, but in fact the current system bears a number of similarities to a free-market economy.

The Chinese people responded positively to the changes. Businessman Robert Lawrence Kuhn describes the results in his book *Made in China,* published in 2000: "By the 1990s, in the full flush of reform, it was a common joke that *all* Chinese people were going into business. 'Jumping into the sea' was the operant metaphor—a phrase that captures the excitement and uncertainty of the market economy." Kuhn also notes that China's economic plan greatly boosted the country's gross domestic product (GDP)—between 1978 and 2002, it quadrupled to reach $6 trillion. China's modernization and improvements in its economy has resulted in a renewed sense of optimism among Chinese people across the country.

However, of those who have been given the chance to better their lives, many have decided they want even more opportunities. As China's huge population has continued to grow, the country's labor market has swelled and job competition has often been very intense. According to some estimates, the surplus labor force of China ranges from 100 million to 250 million. For some of these surplus workers, immigration may be the only way to find work.

Hong Kong and Taiwan

After many decades of being under British rule, the territory of Hong Kong was returned to Chinese control in 1997. Some leaders and journalists in the West feared that there would be violence on the day that Hong Kong changed hands, whether initiated by the soldiers from the People's Republic of China or by the city residents. However, the transition went smoothly, perhaps because in the years before it took place, many who opposed the Communist system had already emigrated from the city.

Deng Xiaoping had described the relationship between Hong Kong and the People's Republic of China as "one country, two systems," assuring the people of Hong Kong that they would continue to benefit from the existing capitalist economic system. However, Hong Kong residents were understandably concerned about their political and civil liberties under China's "one country, two systems" arrangement.

The Chinese government in Beijing has promised Taiwan the same "one country, two systems" plan if it would agree to rejoin mainland China, but the Taiwanese government has expressed no interest in acting on this offer.

Practitioners of Falun Gong meditate in a park in Hong Kong. A public spiritual movement since 1992, Falun Gong was outlawed in China in 1999 and has faced persecution by the authorities for over a decade. Thousands of members of the group have served sentences in prisons and labor camps for practicing the faith.

Lack of Religious Freedom

The People's Republic of China, like many Communist countries, actively discourages its citizens from practicing their religious beliefs. During the Cultural Revolution, Buddhist ancestor-worship shrines were torn apart, and it was made explicitly clear to religious missionaries that they were unwelcome. But for the most part, while persecution of Tibetan Buddhists and some Christian groups has continued, the Chinese government's policy toward religious organizations has been less oppressive than it was decades ago. That attitude changed in the 1990s with the growth of a faith known as Falun Gong.

A public movement in China since 1992, Falun Gong bases its spiritual practice on physical movement to traditional Chinese music and shares some concepts with Taoism, Buddhism, and traditional Chinese thought about the body and medicine. The Chinese government claims that the religion's beliefs about medicine are harmful and socially destabilizing. Falun Gong was labeled a cult by the Chinese government and its practice has been outlawed since 1999. During the 1990s and the early years of the 21st century, the Chinese government imprisoned more than 100,000 practitioners of Falun Gong and sent tens of thousands of others to labor camps without trial.

The Universal Declaration of Human Rights, which China signed along with other members of the United Nations, guarantees basic human rights such as freedom of speech and freedom of belief. However, the People's Republic of China maintains that it has the right to safeguard the stability of its government against movements it considers destructive like the Falun Gong. Practitioners and supporters of the faith believe that freedom of religion is an important human right. They, like Tibetan Buddhists and Chinese Christians, have demonstrated that the search for religious freedom is a motivating factor behind emigration from China.

3 COMING TO AMERICA

Many Chinese in the late 20th century have found that the desires for political, personal, and religious freedom, as well as greater economic opportunities, are powerful incentives to immigrate to the United States and Canada. Although there have been periods of openness in Chinese immigration to North America, the Chinese have also faced major restrictions, particularly in the late 19th and early 20th centuries. To have a general understanding of the motivations behind these restrictions, as well as the policies that have shaped present-day immigration, it is helpful to take a brief look at the history of immigration to the U.S. and Canada.

A Short History of U.S. Immigration

Immigration to the United States has been characterized by openness punctuated by periods of restriction. During the 17th, 18th, and 19th centuries, immigration was essentially open without restriction, and, at times, immigrants were even recruited to come to America. Between 1783 and 1820, approximately 250,000 immigrants arrived at U.S. shores. Between 1841 and 1860, more than 4 million immigrants came; most were from England, Ireland, and Germany.

Historically, race and ethnicity have played a role in legislation to restrict immigration. The Chinese Exclusion Act of 1882, which was not repealed until 1943, specifically prevented Chinese people from becoming U.S. citizens and did not

◀ During the early years of immigration, Chinese immigrants were processed through this station on Angel Island, located in the San Francisco Bay. First put into operation in 1910, this "Ellis Island of the West" was primarily a detention center for entering Chinese whose eligibility as legal immigrants was yet to be determined.

allow Chinese laborers to immigrate for the next decade. An agreement with Japan in the early 1900s prevented most Japanese immigration to the United States.

Until the 1920s, no numerical restrictions on immigration existed in the United States, although health restrictions applied. The only other significant restrictions came in 1917, when passing a literacy test became a requirement for immigrants. Presidents Cleveland, Taft, and Wilson had vetoed similar measures earlier. In addition, in 1917 a prohibition was added to the law against the immigration of people from Asia (defined as the Asiatic barred zone). While a few of these prohibitions were lifted during World War II, they were not repealed until 1952, and even then Asians were only allowed in under very small annual quotas.

U.S. Immigration Policy from World War I to 1965

During World War I, the federal government required that all travelers to the United States obtain a visa at a U.S. consulate or diplomatic post abroad. As former State Department consular affairs officer C. D. Scully points out, by making that requirement permanent Congress, by 1924, established the framework of temporary, or non-immigrant visas (for study, work, or travel), and immigrant visas (for permanent residence). That framework remains in place today.

After World War I, cultural intolerance and bizarre racial theories led to new immigration restrictions. The House Judiciary Committee employed a eugenics consultant, Dr. Harry N. Laughlin, who asserted that certain races were inferior. Another leader of the eugenics movement, Madison Grant, argued that Jews, Italians, and others were inferior because of their supposedly different skull size.

The Immigration Act of 1924, preceded by the Temporary Quota Act of 1921, set new numerical limits on immigration based on "national origin." Taking effect in 1929, the 1924 act set annual quotas on immigrants that were specifically designed

Documenting China's Human Rights Abuses

Born in China in 1937, Harry Hongda Wu came of age while Chairman Mao was implementing his Great Leap Forward programs. In the 1960s, Wu was condemned as a "rightist," and for 19 years was forced to take on backbreaking work in labor camps located throughout the country.

After escaping from China in 1985, Wu moved to the United States. There he gained American citizenship, wrote a revealing autobiography about his prison experience, *Bitter Winds*, and began speaking out about the practices of China's labor camps and other human rights abuses committed by the Chinese government. In his publications, Wu claims that some of the goods exported by China are products of forced labor. During the 1990s, Wu secretly traveled to China, where he continued to gather information on various abuses.

During one such trip in 1995, Wu was caught by the Chinese government and arrested. Although convicted of spying for the American government and sentenced to prison, the Chinese government ultimately returned him to the United States in the interests of maintaining positive diplomatic relations. Wu tried to go back to China in March 2002, but authorities in Hong Kong refused to let him enter the country. He then resumed his life in the United States, where he continues to be a prominent advocate for democracy and human rights in China.

to keep out southern Europeans, such as Italians and Greeks. Generally no more than 100 people of the proscribed nationalities were permitted to immigrate.

While the new law was rigid, the U.S. Department of State's restrictive interpretation directed consular officers overseas to be even stricter in their application of the "public charge" provision. (A public charge is someone unable to support himself or his family.) As author Laura Fermi wrote, "In response to the new cry for restriction at the beginning of the [Great Depression] . . . the consuls were to interpret very strictly the clause prohibiting admission of aliens 'likely to become public charges; and to deny the visa to an applicant who in their opinion might become a public charge at any time.'"

In the early 1900s, more than one million immigrants a year

came to the United States. In 1930—the first year of the national-origin quotas—approximately 241,700 immigrants were admitted. But under the State Department's strict interpretations, only 23,068 immigrants entered during 1933, the smallest total since 1831. Later these restrictions prevented many Jews in Germany and elsewhere in Europe from escaping what would become the Holocaust. At the height of the Holocaust in 1943, the United States admitted fewer than 6,000 refugees.

The Displaced Persons Act of 1948, the nation's first refugee law, allowed many refugees from World War II to settle in the United States. The law put into place policy changes that had already seen immigration rise from 38,119 in 1945 to 108,721 in 1946 (and later to 249,187 in 1950). One-third of those admitted between 1948 and 1951 were Poles, with ethnic Germans forming the second-largest group.

The 1952 Immigration and Nationality Act is best known for

In 1965 President Lyndon Johnson signed the Immigration and Nationality Act, one of the most pivotal immigration laws of the last 50 years. The act provided opportunities to thousands of Chinese and other Asians immigrating to the United States.

its restrictions against those who supported communism or anarchy. However, the bill's other provisions were quite restrictive and were passed over the veto of President Truman. The 1952 act retained the national-origin quota system for the Eastern Hemisphere. The Western Hemisphere continued to operate without a quota and relied on other qualitative factors to limit immigration. Moreover, during that time, the Mexican bracero program, from 1942 to 1964, allowed millions of Mexican agricultural workers to work temporarily in the United States.

The 1952 act set aside half of each national quota to be divided among three preference categories for relatives of U.S. citizens and permanent residents. The other half went to aliens with high education or exceptional abilities. These quotas applied only to those from the Eastern Hemisphere.

A Halt to the National-Origin Quotas

The Immigration and Nationality Act of 1965 became a landmark in immigration legislation by specifically striking the racially based national-origin quotas. It removed the barriers to Asian immigration, which later led to opportunities to immigrate for many Filipinos, Chinese, Koreans, and others. The Western Hemisphere was designated a ceiling of 120,000 immigrants but without a preference system or per country limits. Modifications made in 1978 ultimately combined the Western and Eastern Hemispheres into one preference system and one ceiling of 290,000.

The 1965 act built on the existing system—without the national-origin quotas—and gave somewhat more priority to family relationships. It did not completely overturn the existing system but rather carried forward essentially intact the family immigration categories from the 1959 amendments to the Immigration and Nationality Act. Even though the text of the law prior to 1965 indicated that half of the immigration slots were reserved for skilled employment immigration, in practice, Immigration and Naturalization Service (INS) statistics show that 86 percent of the visas issued between 1952 and 1965 went for family immigration.

A number of significant pieces of legislation since 1980 have shaped the current U.S. immigration system. First, the Refugee Act of 1980 removed refugees from the annual world limit and established that the president would set the number of refugees who could be admitted each year after consultations with Congress.

Second, the 1986 Immigration Reform and Control Act (IRCA) introduced sanctions against employers who "knowingly" hired undocumented immigrants (those here illegally). It also provided amnesty for many undocumented immigrants.

Third, the Immigration Act of 1990 increased legal immigration by 40 percent. In particular, the act significantly increased the number of employment-based immigrants (to 140,000), while also boosting family immigration.

Fourth, the 1996 Illegal Immigration Reform and Immigrant Responsibility Act (IIRAIRA) significantly tightened rules that permitted undocumented immigrants to convert to legal status and made other changes that tightened immigration law in areas such as political asylum and deportation.

Fifth, in response to the September 11, 2001, terrorist attacks, the USA PATRIOT Act and the Enhanced Border Security and Visa Entry Reform Act tightened rules on the granting of visas to individuals from certain countries and enhanced the federal government's monitoring and detention authority over foreign nationals in the United States.

New U.S. Immigration Agencies

In a dramatic reorganization of the federal government, the Homeland Security Act of 2002 abolished the Immigration and Naturalization Service and transferred its immigration service and enforcement functions from the Department of Justice into a new Department of Homeland Security. The Customs Service, the Coast Guard, and parts of other agencies were also transferred into the new department.

President Bush signs the Enhanced Border Security and Visa Entry Reform Act with congressional members in attendance, May 2002. The act, along with the USA PATRIOT Act, was passed in response to the September 2001 terrorist attacks.

The Department of Homeland Security, with regards to immigration, is organized as follows: The Bureau of Customs and Border Protection (BCBP) contains Customs and Immigration inspectors, who check the documents of travelers to the United States at air, sea, and land ports of entry; and Border Patrol agents, the uniformed agents who seek to prevent unlawful entry along the southern and northern border. The new Bureau of Immigration and Customs Enforcement (BICE) employs investigators, who attempt to find undocumented immigrants inside the United States, and Detention and Removal officers, who detain and seek to deport such individuals. The new Bureau of Citizenship and Immigration Services (BCIS) is where people go, or correspond with, to become U.S. citizens or obtain permission to work or extend their stay in the United States.

Following the terrorist attacks of September 11, 2001, the Department of Justice adopted several measures that did not require new legislation to be passed by Congress. Some of these measures created controversy and raised concerns about civil liberties. For example, FBI and INS agents detained for months more than 1,000 foreign nationals of Middle Eastern descent and refused to release the names of the individuals. It is alleged that the Department of Justice adopted tactics that discouraged the detainees from obtaining legal assistance. The Department of Justice also began requiring foreign nationals from primarily Muslim nations to be fingerprinted and questioned by immigration officers upon entry or if they have been living in the United States. Those involved in the September 11 attacks were not immigrants—people who become permanent residents with a right to stay in the United States—but holders of temporary visas, primarily visitor or tourist visas.

Immigration to the United States Today

Today, the annual rate of legal immigration is lower than that at earlier periods in U.S. history. For example, from 1901 to 1910 approximately 10.4 immigrants per 1,000 U.S. residents came to the United States. Today, the annual rate is about 3.5 immigrants per 1,000 U.S. residents. While the percentage of foreign-born people in the U.S. population has risen above 11 percent, it remains lower than the 13 percent or higher that prevailed in the country from 1860 to 1930. Still, as has been the case previously in U.S. history, some people argue that even legal immigration should be lowered. These people maintain that immigrants take jobs native-born Americans could fill and that U.S. population growth, which immigration contributes to, harms the environment. In 1996 Congress voted against efforts to reduce legal immigration.

Most immigrants (800,000 to one million annually) enter the United States legally. But over the years the undocumented (illegal) portion of the population has increased to about 2.8 percent of the U.S. population—approximately 8 million people in all.

Today, the legal immigration system in the United States contains many rules, permitting only individuals who fit into certain categories to immigrate—and in many cases only after waiting anywhere from 1 to 10 years or more, depending on the demand in that category. The system, representing a compromise among family, employment, and human rights concerns, has the following elements:

A U.S. citizen may sponsor for immigration a spouse, parent, sibling, or minor or adult child.

A lawful permanent resident (green card holder) may sponsor only a spouse or child.

A foreign national may immigrate if he or she gains an employer sponsor.

An individual who can show that he or she has a "well-founded fear of persecution" may come to the country as a refugee—or be allowed to stay as an asylee (someone who receives asylum).

Beyond these categories, essentially the only other way to immigrate is to apply for and receive one of the "diversity" visas, which are granted annually by lottery to those from "underrepresented" countries.

In 1996 changes to the law prohibited nearly all incoming

A Chinese man (left) is sworn in as a U.S. citizen during a mass ceremony in New York City. Since the passing of the Immigration and Nationality Act of 1965 and other acts opening up immigration, many more Chinese newcomers have entered the country and have gone on to receive their U.S. citizenship.

immigrants from being eligible for federal public benefits, such as welfare, during their first five years in the country. Refugees were mostly excluded from these changes. In addition, families who sponsor relatives must sign an affidavit of support showing they can financially take care of an immigrant who falls on hard times.

Chinese Immigration to the United States

Early Chinese immigrants to North America were mostly from the southeastern province of Guangdong, although the provinces of Fujian, Zhejiang, and Hainan also sent large numbers of immigrants, a great majority of whom were male.

While male Chinese laborers were encouraged to migrate, in general government officials from China, Canada, and the United States discouraged Chinese families from settling in North America. China wanted to ensure its economy continued to benefit from goods and capital being sent back from North America. And American and Canadian officials wanted to keep the cheap labor working on their railroads and in their gold mines, while deterring ethnic groups from completely assimilating into American society and threatening the status quo.

Those Chinese workers allowed into the United States made great sacrifices. The hours were long and hard, and they suffered from discrimination, which sometimes took the form of violence. In *Strangers from a Different Shore: A History of Asian Americans*, Ronald Takaki listed typical expressions from an English-Chinese phrase book published in 1875. Some of them—"He took it from me by violence" and "He cheated me out of my wages"—reflect the harsh experiences of the Chinese immigrant during that period.

However, the contributions of Chinese Americans during World War II helped change the position of the group in the United States forever. America's entry into the war in December 1941, just after the Japanese attack on Pearl Harbor, was a rallying point for many Chinese Americans. They already considered themselves enemies of Japan, which had attacked and occupied China during the 1930s. With the entry of the United States into the war, both the adopted country of the Chinese Americans and their homeland fought together against a common enemy.

Takaki reports that approximately 22 percent of all adult Chinese American males enlisted in the U.S. armed forces during the Second World War. Many other Chinese—male and female—worked in defense industries. Because there were no designated Chinese American units of the military, the Chinese were integrated into white units. Many American soldiers with European ethnic backgrounds, at first uncomfortable being integrated with minorities, learned to respect Chinese American soldiers as they fought as comrades in arms.

The high enlistment rate of Chinese in the military was the result of the great majority of Chinese American bachelors who were eligible for the draft. After the war, Chinese women were able to immigrate in huge numbers to the United States and Canada as war brides. By the 1960s, the Chinese immigrant population had evened out to approximately the same number of men and women.

In 1965 the People's Republic of China and the United States did not have full diplomatic relations, which meant that immigration was virtually closed. Most Chinese immigrants to the United States came from Hong Kong, which was then a British colony. As a British territory, Hong Kong was permitted to send only 200 immigrants, 1 percent of the "mother country's" quota. However, with the passage of the 1965 Immigration and Nationality Act many eager Chinese scientists and engineers could enter the country. The United States opened its doors to a nonrestricted quota of 20,000 immigrants from China per year, allowing large numbers to come as families.

In 1977, the U.S. regulations governing admissions for technically skilled workers were modified for medical personnel. Beginning that year, only foreign physicians and surgeons who had passed the examination given by the National Board of Medical Examiners could apply for admission into the United

Chinese construction workers take a break to eat their lunch. Many Chinese professionals, especially those in the medicine field, have found that their credentials are not transferable in the U.S. and have thus had to take employment with fewer skill requirements.

States as medical professionals. By the 1980s, this policy had caused a drop in the number of Asian doctors, nurses, and other health care professionals entering the United States under the medical-worker category. Many of these workers came under the family reunification category instead. Once in the United States, some of these immigrants found work as service or factory workers because their medical credentials weren't transferable.

From the mid-1960s to the mid-1970s, about half the arriving immigrants from China were low-skilled workers such as clerks, craftsmen, and service workers. The other half consisted of professionals and more high-skilled workers. The demographic makeup of Chinese Americans in the United States changed significantly during this period. Many entered prestigious occupations, now acknowledged as the bright people of high ability they were rather than people to be saddled with the most menial labor. In fact, several Nobel Prize–winners came from this generation of Chinese Americans.

A Short History of Canadian Immigration

In the 1800s, immigration into Canada was largely unrestricted. Farmers and artisans from England and Ireland made up a significant portion of 19th-century immigrants. England's Parliament passed laws that facilitated and encouraged the voyage to North America, particularly for the poor.

After the United States barred Chinese railroad workers from settling in the country, Canada encouraged the immigration of Chinese laborers to assist in the building of Canadian railways. Responding to the racial views of the time, the Canadian Parliament began charging a "head tax" for Chinese and South Asian (Indian) immigrants in 1885. The fee of $50—later raised to $500—was well beyond the means of laborers making one or two dollars a day. Later, the government sought additional ways to prohibit Asians from entering the country. For example, it decided to require a "continuous journey," meaning that immigrants to Canada had to travel from their country on a boat that made an uninterrupted passage. For immigrants or asylum seekers from Asia this was nearly impossible.

As the 20th century progressed, concerns about race led to further restrictions on immigration to Canada. These restrictions particularly hurt Jewish and other refugees seeking to flee persecution in Europe. Government statistics indicate that Canada accepted no more than 5,000 Jewish refugees before and during the Holocaust.

After World War II, Canada, like the United States, began accepting thousands of Europeans displaced by the war. Canada's laws were modified to accept these war refugees, as well as Hungarians fleeing Communist authorities after the crushing of the 1956 Hungarian Revolution.

The Immigration Act of 1952 in Canada allowed for a "tap on, tap off" approach to immigration, granting administrative authorities the power to allow more immigrants into the country in good economic times, and fewer in times of recession. The shortcoming of such an approach is that there is little evidence immigrants harm a national economy and much evidence they contribute to economic growth, particularly in the growth of the labor force.

In 1966 the government of Prime Minister Lester Pearson introduced a policy statement stressing how immigrants were key to Canada's economic growth. With Canada's relatively small population base, it became clear that in the absence of newcomers, the country would not be able to grow. The policy was introduced four years after Parliament enacted important legislation that eliminated Canada's own version of racially based national-origin quotas.

In 1967 a new law established a points system that awarded entry to potential immigrants using criteria based primarily on an individual's age, language ability, skills, education, family relationships, and job prospects. The total points needed for entry of an immigrant is set by the Minister of Citizenship and Immigration Canada. The new law also established a category for humanitarian (refugee) entry.

The 1976 Immigration Act refined and expanded the possibility for entry under the points system, particularly for those seeking to sponsor family members. The act also expanded refugee and asylum law to comport with Canada's international obligations. The law established five basic categories for immigration into Canada: 1) family; 2) humanitarian; 3) independents (including skilled workers), who immigrate to Canada on their own; 4) assisted relatives; and 5) business immigrants (including investors, entrepreneurs, and the self-employed).

The new Immigration and Refugee Protection Act, which took effect June 28, 2002, made a series of modifications to existing Canadian immigration law. The act, and the regulations that followed, toughened rules on those seeking asylum and the process for removing people unlawfully in Canada.

The law modified the points system, adding greater flexibility for skilled immigrants and temporary workers to become permanent residents, and evaluating skilled workers on the weight of their transferable skills as well as those of their specific occupation. The legislation also made it easier for employers to have a labor shortage declared in an industry or sector, which would facilitate the entry of foreign workers in that industry or sector.

On family immigration, the act permitted parents to sponsor dependent children up to the age of 22 (previously 19 was the maximum age at which a child could be sponsored for immigration). The act also allowed partners in common-law arrangements, including same-sex partners, to be considered as family members for the purpose of immigration sponsorship. Along with these liberalizing measures, the act also included provisions to address perceived gaps in immigration-law enforcement.

Chinese Immigration to Canada

After World War II, Canadian immigration policy dictated that the Chinese share the same immigrant category—"of Asiatic origin"—with the Japanese. This meant that although China had been an ally of Canada during the war, the Chinese were restricted from immigrating to Canada. Some Canadian

A boy shows his Canadian pride at a Chinese New Year parade. In the years between World War II and the halt to national-origin quotas in 1967, potential Chinese immigrants to Canada were faced with many imposing restrictions.

politicians were opposed to admitting more "Asiatics" into the country, even those who were relatives of Canadian citizens. The Canadian Citizenship Act of 1947 allowed the wives and children of citizens and legal residents of Canada to enter the country, but there was a specific clause that excluded "immigrants of any Asiatic race" from this provision.

Many Canadian Chinese, especially members of the Chinese Benevolent Association of Canada, lobbied to change such immigration laws, but the gap between the number of Chinese people and the number of other immigrants allowed to enter the country only widened. It was not until 1967 that Canadian legislators finally lifted restrictions based on nationality, ethnic group, class, or area of origin.

Anthony Chan, an expert on Chinese immigration to Canada, observed in his book *Gold Mountain* that throughout the history of early Chinese immigration, many newcomers felt ties to the general continent of North America rather than to the individual nations of Canada or the United States. Chan wrote:

> [A] Vancouver cannery worker writing to his peasant family in Taishan would not refer to Canada but to Gold Mountain, just as another family in the same district might hear from their relatives in San Francisco who would talk of Gold Mountain but not about *Meiguo* (America).

> Racist attitudes of the white population helped crystallize Chinese North America into a cohesive community, but perhaps the strongest glue was the community's passionate interest in the affairs and politics of China.

U.S.–China Relations

Of particular concern for Chinese immigrants was the issue of how China's political system could continue to make immigration difficult for friends and family still living in the homeland. So much depended on the state of diplomatic relations between the North American countries and China. Canada did not recognize the Communist government in Beijing as legitimate until the early 1970s, while the United States only recognized the British colony city of Hong Kong and the Nationalist government in Taiwan for most of the 1960s and 1970s. As a result, anyone who wanted to legally immigrate from the People's Republic of China to the United States had to first get to Taiwan or Hong Kong.

Full diplomatic relations between the United States and Communist China were finally established in 1979, and three years later, the People's Republic of China was permitted to send immigrants to the United States, under the conditions of the 20,000-per-country limit that applied to other Eastern Hemisphere countries. In recognition of the new diplomatic relations between the United States and China, the U.S. government pledged it would not interfere in the affairs between China and Taiwan, although Taiwan was given a separate immigration quota by special amendment.

Although the United States had established diplomatic relations with the People's Republic of China, the U.S. government remained concerned about China's ongoing human rights violations. The events in Tiananmen Square in 1989 prompted the administration of President George H. W. Bush to allow Chinese citizens who had entered the United States before the massacre to remain in the country. This action benefited Chinese students, tourists, and people with temporary work visas. The Chinese Student Adjustment Act of 1992 helped many of these individuals become permanent residents and, if they wanted, U.S. citizens.

Those who could not legally leave China found other ways to emigrate. The 1990s saw growing numbers of undocumented Chinese immigrants leave the country. Those who were caught were usually deported back to China.

4 FROM CHINATOWN TO THE SUBURBS

Chinese immigrants tend to settle in the same regions of the United States and Canada, a pattern that has resulted in the creation of large Chinese neighborhoods. Many major North American cities, as well as smaller cities and suburbs, now have well-established Chinese communities.

Chinese American and Chinese Canadian Enclaves

The Pacific coastal cities—Los Angeles and San Francisco, California; Seattle, Washington; and Vancouver, British Columbia—have long appealed to Chinese immigrants for their proximity to the homeland. Chinese American communities developed in these cities long ago, in the days when Chinese immigrants arrived on the West Coast by way of a ship journey across the Pacific Ocean. Today more than half of the Chinese in the United States live in the Pacific states. A large segment also lives in Hawaii, which since the second half of the 19th century has had a particularly high Asian population. Hawaii's communities include many Chinese Americans and Americans of mixed ethnicity.

Although the earliest Chinese immigrants made their homes in the West, many others eventually settled in regions across the United States. A large number of Chinese immigrants live on the East Coast (particularly in New York, New Jersey, and Massachusetts) and in the Midwest (Illinois, Michigan, and

◀The streets of Chinatown neighborhoods often come alive as bustling marketplaces. Many Chinese immigrants choose to settle in Chinatown neighborhoods, which are found in many major cities of North America, including San Francisco, New York, Philadelphia, and Toronto.

Ohio). The majority have settled in cultural enclaves, typically called Chinatown, located within or just outside the major cities.

Chinatowns consist primarily of housing and businesses that serve the Chinese community. Such enterprises typically include Chinese restaurants and teahouses, jewelry stores, beauty salons, retail stores, open-air markets, professional offices, and garment manufacturers. Often popular with tourists, Chinatowns are filled with restaurants that introduce other ethnic groups to Chinese food and culture. These enclaves also serve as an entry point for many newcomers, who find the

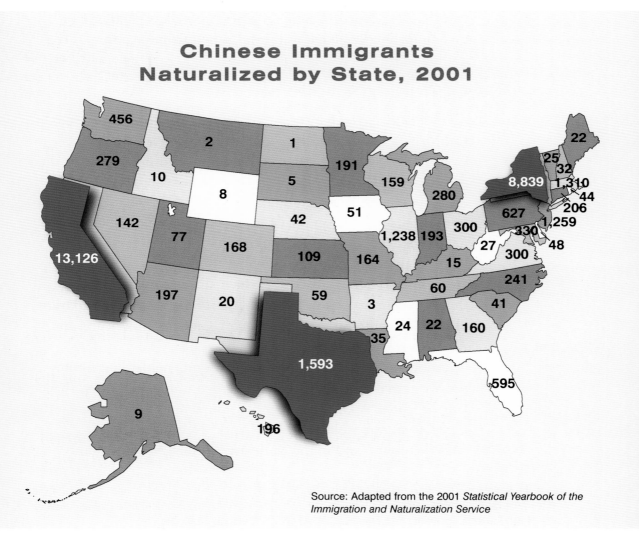

Chinese Immigrants Naturalized by State, 2001

Source: Adapted from the 2001 *Statistical Yearbook of the Immigration and Naturalization Service*

Vancouver, British Columbia, is a popular place to settle for Chinese immigrants to Canada. Like other major cities on the Pacific coast, Vancouver has a Chinatown that was originally established during the 19th century.

transition to life in the United States or Canada easier to handle among people who speak their language.

New York City contains the largest Chinese population outside Asia. During the second half of the 20th century, the city's Chinese population exploded, growing from about 33,000 in 1960, to around 240,000 in 1990, to more than 360,000 in 2000. Today, the Chinese are the largest Asian group in the city of New York, making up 46 percent of all Asians in its five boroughs. The area's dominant language is Cantonese, as immigrants from all over China, but especially South China, have clustered there. Population reports indicate that most immigrants from China's Fujian province end up living in New York City.

New York actually features two major Chinatowns—one that is squeezed into a two-square-mile area of the lower East Side of the Manhattan borough, and the other located in Flushing, Queens, where large numbers of Taiwanese immigrants began congregating in the 1970s. These Mandarin-speaking Chinese sometimes refer to the region as "Little Taipei," after the capital city of Taiwan.

Other popular Chinatown districts can be found in the cities of San Francisco, Chicago, Boston, Philadelphia, Houston, Vancouver, and Toronto. As increased Chinese immigration has attracted more and more newcomers, the borders of most major metropolitan Chinatowns have expanded, and Chinese communities have naturally spilled outside the boundaries of Chinatown and into suburban enclaves.

A sense of community is very important to the Chinese people, so the Chinatowns and similar neighborhoods have served to put new immigrants in familiar situations, with institutions they already know and trust. Many Chinese immigrants have relied upon the Chinatown social networks for assistance in beginning their new lives.

Business Owners and Professional Workers

Chinese Americans are renowned for their skills in starting up and running successful small businesses. Many immigrants become entrepreneurs, organizing and managing their own businesses. These may be small stores, restaurants, or service businesses such as dry cleaners or laundries.

For the early Chinese immigrants to North America, racial discrimination was a crucial factor behind job availability. Because the Chinese were prohibited from becoming citizens, owning land, voting, or holding public office during the early 20th century, many were excluded from major areas of employment in the general economy. In the established white communities, a large number of Chinese found work by opening their own laundries and restaurant businesses.

Even for those with college degrees, employment opportunities were very limited. In the 1940s, a Stanford University report observed that it was almost impossible during that time to place a Chinese or Japanese graduate in a position, whether in engineering, manufacturing, or business. Chinese Americans with bachelor's degrees and even advanced degrees and who spoke excellent English sometimes found themselves working as servants just so they could feed their families back home.

Today, it is fairly typical for Chinese newcomers to work in a handful of industries that are friendly toward speakers of Chinese dialects. These industries include restaurants, Chinese

"Chinese" versus "Asian American" or "Asianadian"

Recent immigrants have trouble understanding how an ethnic Chinese person can identify himself or herself simply as Asian American or Asianadian (Asian Canadian). After all, Chinese people generally distinguish themselves from the Japanese, Koreans, and other Asian ethnic groups, each of which has its own distinct language and culture. However, in North America many Chinese, Japanese, Vietnamese, and other Asian groups often find that they have been lumped together as one ethnic entity and treated similarly. Some Asians have taken something positive from this generalization, as it has forced them to acknowledge the political concerns that they have in common. Hate crimes, although relatively rare, is one particular issue on which Asian groups have come together.

One famous hate-crime incident occurred on June 19, 1982, when a Chinese American man named Vincent Chin was murdered in Detroit, Michigan. Two white unemployed autoworkers, who blamed the then-booming Japanese auto industry for the loss of their jobs, mistakenly identified Chin as Japanese. While uttering ethnic slurs, they cornered him in an alley and savagely beat him to death. In a plea bargain, the two men received a punishment of three years' probation and a fine of $3,780.

This sentence outraged many in the Chinese American community, and they rallied to protest. Many other Asian ethnic groups joined them. In a rare instance of solidarity, some Chinese Americans acknowledged their commonality with Japanese Americans and Korean Americans. The idea of Asian Americans working together on issues gained more credence as a result of Vincent Chin's tragic death.

Seven years later, when a young Chinese American named Ming Hai "Jim" Loo was killed by racists who mistakenly thought he was Vietnamese, members of the Asian American communities were prepared. They were organized, well funded, and ready to protest to make sure that others didn't suffer the same injustice that Vincent Chin's family encountered years before.

or other Asian import stores, and the garment trade (notably clothing manufacture). Educated Chinese immigrants can also find employment in many other fields, including engineering, investment, architecture, insurance, law, and fashion design and entertainment. They have been accepted in many more fields in recent years than they were from the 1930s to the 1950s, with more respectable and highly paid occupations available to them. However, it is sometimes necessary for medical professionals trained in China to take other jobs while they undergo the certification process to practice in the United States.

The skills that Chinese immigrants hold before their journey to North America have a significant impact on the kind of work they end up doing in their new country. Those who were educated in technical fields or who speak English well can frequently obtain white-collar, professional jobs and can more easily assimilate into mainstream American culture.

Many Chinese Americans are finding success today as white-collar professionals and small business owners. Immigrants of past generations did not have the same financial success, often because they were denied the basic rights enjoyed by U.S. citizens and thus excluded from many job fields.

Better Pay in America

Wages in the United States tend to be much higher than those in China, even with the poorest and most unskilled jobs. When asked by immigration expert Marlowe Hood why he had come to America, Chen Yuan, a Chinese immigrant from the city of Fuzhou, replied:

> When the income differential between China and the United States is 1:2 rather than 1:15 or 1:20, that is when Fuzhounese will stop going and even start to come back. . . . Look at it this way—in terms of income potential for the average worker, one year [of work] in the United States equals 15 Chinese years.

Chinese immigration researcher Ko-Lin Chin made a similar discovery when he studied a group of 300 undocumented Fujianese immigrants. In his book *Smuggled Chinese: Clandestine Immigration to the United States*, he reported his survey results: "About 61 percent of my respondents said they came to the United States for only one reason—to make money. Another 25 percent stated that their primary motive was to make money but also mentioned one or more nonmonetary reasons for coming." Some survey respondents reported that they made less than $30 a year in China. Coming from such extreme poverty, these Chinese immigrants view even the poorest American workers as making startling amounts of money.

People who grew up in the grinding poverty still prevalent in some parts of China are sometimes astonished by such American "basics" as paved roads and access to electricity. Even wealthy immigrants who have moved from China's cities find the wages and standard of living in North America to be much higher than that of China.

In a 1997 study of Asian American men and wages, researchers Arthur Sakamoto and Jeng Liu found that on average Chinese male immigrants earned about 16 percent less than white men, but that U.S.–born Chinese men earned about 6 percent more. Although other experts disagree with these findings, according to the 2000 U.S. Census Asian Americans had

the highest median household income ($51,400) of any foreign-born or native group in the United States.

The high education level of Chinese Americans helps to explain the high income of Asian Americans. Using data from 1990, Sakamoto and Liu reported that 33 percent of Chinese American men held a bachelor's degree, as compared to only 17 percent of white men. An impressive 12 percent of Chinese American men had obtained a Ph.D. or professional degree, while only 4 percent of white men accomplished that feat.

Problems Facing Immigrant Laborers

Many recent Chinese immigrants have arrived in America in debt. In order to pay back passage fees from China, as well as day-to-day living expenses, they have to work constantly, often finding little time for their families. Some Chinese immigrants find jobs in Chinatown garment factories making less than minimum wage. They are typically paid per piece of work

A Chinese worker in a Chinatown fish market presents fresh crabs for sale. Because the average wage level in the United States and Canada is so much higher than in China, many immigrants are attracted primarily by the promise of higher income.

rather than at an hourly rate. In her book *Chinatown: A Portrait of a Closed Society*, Gwen Kinkead reported:

> In the four Chinatown shops I visited, everyone put in at least sixty hours a week, some for less than $200. A handful earned over $300. The majority made about $4 an hour, slightly less than burger flippers in McDonald's working nine to five at minimum wage—$4.25 an hour [at the time]. . . . When the piece rates drop below union minimums, or minimum wage, workers silently knuckle under and try to recover the lost wages by working even longer hours.

Many Chinese immigrant women who do not speak English find work as seamstresses in the garment industry. A study of garment workers in San Francisco's Chinatown found that 72 percent of the workers were women whose husbands were also working but in other fields, mostly in the restaurant business.

The differences between the employment of Chinese American men and women are not surprising, considering the employment standards of China. While the Communist government officially considers men and women to be equal, traditional Chinese families often value sons more than daughters and treat women with less respect. In general the responsibility for most of the housework and family care still falls upon women. The attitudes of Chinese women toward the American ideal of gender equality are greatly influenced by their education and where they live.

First-generation Chinese Americans and Immigrant Children

First-generation Chinese Americans and immigrant children who are fluent in English sometimes find themselves in the position of having to run the house or take care of parents who have limited English skills. This situation in which children are in the position of family responsibility runs counter to Chinese custom, in which the elder members have near-complete authority. Such change in the family structure often causes great stress for older immigrants.

Some children have difficulty acclimating to life in their new homeland because they immigrate many years after their parents. Such children may have spent years in China or Taiwan, where they were raised by grandparents until their parents could afford to send for them. In her book *Teenage Refugees from China Speak Out*, Colleen She interviewed Yi-Hua, a young girl who immigrated from Beijing long after her parents' arrival:

> My immigration here was planned by my parents. I have been separated from them for nearly ten years. It is difficult to come to a strange land and live with parents you did not grow up with. I feel that getting reacquainted with my parents will be my greatest challenge.

Transitions for children like Yi-Hua can be especially difficult. Not only have they been deprived of those months and years

A woman teaches her mother how to use a personal data organizer. In many households, the children of Chinese immigrants become more assimilated to American culture and more familiar with the English language; as a result, they may take on a greater decision-making role.

with their parents, but they also are challenged to form new relationships both within and outside the family in their strange new country.

Chinese American Organizations

Chinese immigrants can turn to various groups for help and guidance in acclimating to their new culture. These include family associations, or social service groups such as the Chinese-American Planning Council, which evolved in the late 1960s and 1970s. Services offered by the organization include job training, legal advice, health care, day care, and translation. Family associations also provide care for elders and those in distress.

Unlike many European American immigrants who turn to Christian churches or Jewish synagogues for assistance in settling into their new homeland, Chinese immigrants typically do not depend on religious institutions for support. After decades of Communist rule, some are not religious at all, and those who are tend to worship in the home, usually through ancestor worship (meditation or paying respects to deceased family members). There is, however, a minority population of Chinese immigrant Christians. They often participate in activities provided by Chinese churches in the United States, such as youth fellowship clubs, women's guilds, and education and English classes for new immigrants.

Another well-established Chinese group that helps new immigrants is the Six Companies. The organization evolved from early immigrant groups called *huiguan*, the Cantonese word for "meeting hall." Years ago, Chinese people would gather together in meeting halls to provide each other with mutual support and help in their personal lives as well as in their businesses. Gradually, these social organizations came to be called "companies." Over the years the many companies consolidated and in 1862 became the Chinese Consolidated Benevolent Association, more commonly known as the Chinese Six Companies. This association helps new immigrants find employment and housing, and also provides social opportunities for its members. The organization has also been known to give business loans and help members who have fallen into debt.

Another community support group for the Chinese is the *tongxianghui* (native-place organization). This kind of social network, which first existed in China, welcomes people who are related and/or come from the same place. For much of Chinese American history, most place-based associations were Cantonese and were comprised of people from the Guangdong Province, located in southeast China. Members of the Cantonese *tongxianghui* in America typically allied themselves with China's Nationalist movement during the first half of the 20th century. As anti-Communists, they strongly supported the Nationalist government in Taiwan.

Beginning in the 1990s, the majority of immigrants from China—both legal and undocumented—formed their own community associations, such as the United Chinese Associations of New York, the Fukien American Association, the United Fujianese of American Association, and the American Fujian Association of Commerce and Industry. Unlike earlier organizations, which were fiercely anti-Communist, many of the newer associations were officially pro-Communist.

Yet another kind of Chinese association is the family-name organization, made up of members with the same last name. Some groups combine with others to form larger organizations. For example, the Four Brothers Association is a multifamily benevolent organization that for a small yearly fee grants membership to anyone with the name Quan or one of the group's three other surnames. The association provides free dinners for members, burials for members without family, and other services.

Tongs are groups that were originally formed as benevolent protective associations to help protect the interests of the Chinese community, particularly in dealing with unfair and discriminatory laws. Although there are tongs today that are legitimate associations, others have been known to be associated with organized crime, even if not all their members are criminals. Some law-abiding Chinese join tongs for a variety of reasons, such as for protection or to obtain payments for debts.

One of the largest associations in New York's Chinatown is the Chinese Consolidated Benevolent Organization (CCBA), which runs schools and fosters programs to preserve Chinese culture. A politically conservative and somewhat self-protective organization, the CCBA focuses mostly on supporting Taiwan in its political struggle against the People's Republic of China.

Membership in Chinese American associations such as the CCBA provides new immigrants with a support system that guides their entry into the established community. However, membership in such groups does not always ensure harmony. Some American-born Chinese (nicknamed "ABCs") may believe they have little in common with recent immigrants, who are sometimes derogatively referred to as "fresh off the boat," or "FOBs."

Preserving Chinese Heritage and Identity

Since the mid-1970s many Chinese Americans and Chinese Canadians have become interested in the cultural history of earlier generations. Some Chinese living in North America have formed or joined groups that work to preserve accounts of their past.

Formed in 1981, the Chinese Canadian National Council (originally the Chinese Canadian National Council for Equality), or CCNC, sponsors activities that are mainly apolitical. The organization focuses on maintaining the historical and cultural aspects of the Canadian Chinese. Specifically, it gathers historical artifacts, organizes an annual heritage exhibition and festival, sponsors a scholarship fund in Chinese Canadian studies, and promotes cooperation among various ethnic, cultural, and civil liberties associations. By furthering education about Chinese Canadians, the CCNC hopes to increase awareness

A Chinese Catholic priest stands in front of a cathedral. Because religious practice is repressed in China, only a small segment of the Chinese immigrant population turns to churches and other religious institutions for support during the resettlement process.

and understanding of the unique contributions that Chinese Canadians have made to the larger society. In the United States, groups like the Chinese Historical Society of America and the Chinese Culture Foundation follow a similar agenda.

Many other groups exist in the United States to help bring Chinese Americans together. The Organization of Chinese Americans, which consists mostly of U.S. citizens and permanent residents, works to foster public awareness of the needs and rights of Chinese Americans and advance their responsibilities and opportunities. The organization sponsors social activities such as exhibitions and festivals, as well as educational programs such as cultural and political seminars.

5 BLENDING TRADITIONS

The degree to which Chinese Americans assimilate into Western society varies widely. Some Chinese Americans feel strongly about holding onto their Chinese culture and traditions. Others are willing to give up as many Chinese traits as possible to seem thoroughly American. However, many—perhaps most—prefer to maintain some Chinese traditions while dropping others as they assimilate into American culture and share some of their Chinese heritage with other Americans.

Growing Up in America

Whether a person grows up in Chinese or American society will affect many aspects of his or her behavior, says a Chinese American interviewee who discussed his viewpoint in *Asian American Experiences in the United States* by Joann Faung Jean Lee. He believes that the Chinese person raised in China will differ significantly from the same person raised in Western society. Citing behavioral differences as an example, he explained to Lee that Asians raised in America tend to be more aggressive and less formal than Asians who grew up in Asia. He identifies other differences:

> Asian Americans dress the American way. Whereas Asian[s], regardless of how long they've been here, are basically Asian in look and dress. I don't know how to describe it, but there is some subtle difference, and I can tell. There is a difference in the way they comb their hair, their gestures and the types of clothes

◀ It is common to light incense candles during traditional holidays like the Chinese New Year, which has some celebrations lasting an entire month. Many Chinese Americans light candles during the New Year in memory of their father's ancestors.

they wear. When I was in college, I had trouble getting accepted by Asian Americans. I also had trouble getting accepted by Chinese from Hong Kong. . . . It was not that they wouldn't accept me, but there was a barrier. . . . Since most of them came from Hong Kong, there was a common bond, and I became an outsider.

After years of living in North America, many Chinese Americans develop their own culture, which consists of a blend of elements from both Chinese and Western cultures. This is particularly evident in the rituals and traditions of special occasions. Rather than dropping the traditions of their ancestors or slighting those of their new country, Chinese Americans often use both.

Author Ben Fong-Torres provides an example of this blending of cultures in *The Rice Room: Growing Up Chinese-American from Number Two Son to Rock 'N' Roll*. In the book he remembers attending a Chinese American wedding that incorporated Western and Eastern elements. The bride and groom exchanged vows in a Western-style church, and they were carried out in English, but other rituals reflected many Eastern traditions. The wedding reception consisted of a lavish Chinese banquet. The traditional Chinese dishes were served: roast duck and shark fin soup, which according to tradition represent power and prosperity. The honored guests made toasts in both English and Chinese.

Keeping the Chinese Heritage

Some Chinese families do not make complete assimilation into Western society their primary goal. Traditional Chinese families, fearing that their children and grandchildren will lose their heritage, may pressure them to only marry other Chinese or Chinese Americans. Researcher Betty Lee Sung, who studied the attitudes and experiences of the Chinese regarding intermarriage and integration, noted that in some cases those who did marry outside the Chinese community were not accepted by their families and Chinese friends—even after 30 to 40 years of marriage.

One Chinese immigrant who had to deal with others' disapproval of her interracial marriage was Sue Jean Lee Suettinger, who was interviewed for the book *Asian American Experiences in the United States*. When Suettinger, who came to the United States as a small child, chose to marry a man who was not Chinese, she encountered much negative pressure from her family. In fact, during the six months leading to the wedding, her father refused to speak to her. It was only after the wedding that she made peace with her family, but in the interview she admitted there were consequences to marrying someone of a

(Above) A Chinese New Year parade in Washington, D.C., features a dragon dance. Animal costume dances, featuring two or more dancers, are a key element of every New Year celebration. (Right) A child in costume and makeup performs during another celebration.

different ethnic background, one of which was that her children did not learn to speak Chinese. It is likely that Suettinger's children will want to learn more about China at some point. Second- and third-generation Chinese Americans often feel curious about the land of their ancestors, as do Americans from many different ethnic groups.

Author Maxine Hong Kingston, the daughter of a Chinese immigrant, discusses in her 1980 book *China Men* how she really wanted to see her parents' homeland, but was also concerned about the difficulties that such a visit might involve:

> I'd like to go to China if I can get a visa and—more difficult—permission from my family, who are afraid that applying for a visa would call attention to us: the relatives in China would get in trouble for having American capitalist connections, and we Americans would be put in relocation camps during the next witch hunt for Communists.

However, it should be noted that since U.S.–Chinese relations have improved it has become possible for many later-generation Americans to return to the country their parents left. This group now has more freedom to visit distant relatives or merely see the sights.

Celebrating Holiday Traditions and Customs

Many Westerners are familiar with the Chinese New Year, also called the Spring Festival. Since traditional Chinese culture follows the lunar calendar, the Chinese New Year is celebrated on different dates of the Western calendar. It falls on the first day of the first month of the lunar year, which usually is anytime between late January and early February. The Chinese New Year celebrates the birth of spring and new beginnings, marking a time of renewed hope for a successful future. Considered the most important of Chinese American holidays, the New Year features celebrations that can last for a month.

Before the New Year arrives, people thoroughly clean their homes, buy new clothes, and get haircuts so that they start off the year looking their best. Homes are decorated with good-

The Year of the Zodiac

Like many other Asian groups, the Chinese use the lunar calendar, which bases its months on the changing phases of the moon. According to the Chinese Zodiac, each lunar year (consisting of twelve months) is represented by one of twelve animals, so that the Chinese New Year introduces the Year of the Rat, Ox, Tiger, Hare, Dragon, Snake, Horse, Sheep, Monkey, Rooster, Dog, or Pig. Some people believe that individuals will have the characteristics of the animal representing the year in which he or she was born. For example, someone born in the Year of the Horse is said to be hardworking, honest, independent, and sociable.

In 1993 the U.S. Postal Service began to honor the Chinese New Year with a series of Lunar New Year stamps. Designed by Clarence Lee, this commemorative series started with the Year of the Rooster (1993), and was then followed by the Year of the Dog (1994), Boar (1995), Rat (1996), Ox (1997), Tiger (1998), Hare (1999), Dragon (2000), Snake (2001), Horse (2002), Sheep (2003), and Monkey (2004). The Lunar New Year stamp project was first proposed by members of the Organization of Chinese Americans (OCA).

luck poems written in Chinese characters and a pine bough money tree adorned with coins and paper flowers. Because the Chinese consider the color red to be extremely lucky, they often use it for decorations, particularly during the Chinese New Year.

On the day of the New Year, Chinese families gather together to share feasts and exchange gifts. As part of the celebration, older relatives give children a "lucky red envelope" containing money. Called "Hong Bao" in Chinese, the red color of this traditional gift is thought to contain positive power and thus bring good luck both to the giver and the receiver of the gift.

New Year is also a time to honor one's ancestors for some traditional Chinese families. They keep an altar in the home that features the names of the father's family members going back for several generations. During the New Year holiday, family members place food offerings on the altar, light incense, and bow in honor of their ancestors.

In addition to having ceremonies in the home, family-name

groups and social associations also get together to celebrate the major festivals. In cities where these groups are large, they have been known to host big restaurant dinners for the Chinese New Year. The Chinatowns in major cities often bring in the New Year by hosting parades and setting off fireworks.

Chinese New Year parades usually feature the lion dance, a costumed performance that is thought to bring good fortune and joy to the spectators as well as the performers. The tradition of the lion dance started during the Han dynasty, about 2,000 years ago, and is similar to Taiwanese and Korean dances. Often mistaken by Westerners as a dragon costume, the lion costume requires just two dancers. (The dragon dance,

Children participate in a Lantern Festival parade running through New York's Chinatown, 1960. During the Lantern Festival, which is held on the 15th day of the new lunar month, attendants parade through the streets with lanterns.

which may also be performed at parades, involves more than two people.) One person dances as the head of the lion, controlling its facial expressions to indicate happiness or anger, while the other dances as the tail. Three musical performers, playing the drum, cymbals, and gong, accompany the dancers.

The Chinese New Year festivities last until the 15th day of the new lunar month, and end with the Lantern Festival. This holiday features lantern exhibits, lion and dragon dances, and the serving of boiled sweet rice dumplings called *tang yuan*.

Another important Chinese holiday is Qing Ming, which falls in early spring, often during the first part of April. Its name literally means "the clear and bright festival." On Qing Ming, traditional Chinese families honor their dead ancestors. Traditional celebrations involve cleaning family gravesites or places set aside to remember family members. After the graves are cleaned, some people leave offerings of food and paper replicas of money to their ancestors. Other families celebrate in a less-solemn fashion by having picnics, flying kites, and decorating with flower garlands.

The Autumn Moon Festival, which falls on the 15th day of the 8th lunar month (usually in September), is second only to the Chinese New Year in significance. Sometimes called the Mid-Autumn Festival, the holiday marks the end of the summer harvest and is a time for giving thanks. The Autumn Moon Festival occurs around the time of the autumnal equinox, when the moon appears to be at its largest and brightest.

Families celebrate the holiday by gathering together and holding feasts, which include an abundance of fruits and "moon cakes"—palm-sized round cakes traditionally made with a sweet bean-paste filling. In the center of the cake is a golden egg yoke that looks like a bright moon. Chinatowns often host Moon Festivals featuring arts and crafts displays, food and drink booths, parades, and live entertainment by dancers, acrobats, and martial artists.

Although in China this holiday has a separate designated date for families to reunite and have large dinners, in the United

The Physical Comedy of Jackie Chan

Many Americans are longtime fans of kung fu movies, which feature the Chinese method of unarmed combat that uses hands, elbows, knees, or feet to strike blows. In the past, kung fu films were seldom viewed by a mass audience—that is until Hong Kong martial arts star Jackie Chan used the venue to establish a successful action-comedy career with a following spanning two continents.

Born Chan Kong-Sang in 1954, just after his parents had fled to Hong Kong from the Shangdong province, Chan entered a family that was struggling with poverty. He has told interviewers that his parents were so poor that they almost asked the doctor who delivered Chan to adopt him.

At the age of six, Chan attended the Chinese Drama Academy. After growing up and becoming a working professional, he earned a reputation in the film business, first as a stuntman and then as an actor who did his own stunts. Like his predecessor, kung fu legend Bruce Lee, Jackie Chan eventually made the transition from Hong Kong star to American movie idol. In 2002 he received a star on the Hollywood Walk of Fame.

In his movies, Chan often addresses the culture clash between Westerners and Chinese, making Americans laugh while at the same time they reconsider their assumptions about Eastern cultures. Some of his movies also deal with popular Asian American themes and issues. For instance, the plot of his 1996 film, *Rumble in the Bronx*, involves a clashing rivalry between tong bosses in New York's Chinatown.

States and Canada such festivities occur more commonly during the Chinese New Year or during American holidays such as Thanksgiving, when most family members can get time off from work.

The date that Chinese immigrants celebrate China's national

holiday varies depending on the ethnic makeup of the particular community. Every year, the Cantonese populations of Chinatowns celebrate on October 10, which is the national holiday of Taiwan's Nationalist government. The Cantonese do not acknowledge October 1, which is the Communist national holiday, although the Fujianese communities generally consider that day the proper time for celebrations. Many Chinese American people skip these two dates altogether and throw themselves wholeheartedly into celebrating American holidays such as Independence Day, Canada Day, or Thanksgiving.

Celebrations of certain American-style holidays have sometimes startled new immigrants, although most of them—especially the children—quickly learn to adapt. Ben Fong-Torres recalled his mother's first encounter with Halloween:

> Two months after her arrival in Oakland, my mother was home one evening when her doorbell rang. She pulled back the curtain on the front door window and found herself confronted by two children—one a ghost, the other a witch. Even though they were clearly children, they frightened Mom, and she hurried to the telephone to call Grace Fung [her close friend].
>
> "What is this?" she asked. "Children in make-believe clothes at my front door!"

But soon, like many other immigrants, Fong-Torres's mother was dressing her children up to go trick-or-treating, only weeks after she served them moon cakes for the Harvest Moon Festival.

6 TONGS AND TROUBLES

Any group of immigrants trying to make its way in an established ethnic enclave, and beyond that a larger, more integrated community, will face some difficulties. Recent Chinese immigrants are no exception. Their problems run across a wide spectrum, including labor exploitation, threats from tongs, language barriers in receiving medical and social services, and discrimination. Many of these problems are exacerbated by the large number of undocumented immigrants who come from China to the United States every year.

Illegal Immigration from China

No one is quite sure how many undocumented Chinese immigrants arrive in the United States each year. Some enter the country as virtual indentured servants for the people who smuggled them. Other newcomers have more mobility, but they still try to remain anonymous by not seeking government-funded medical services or help from government or charitable organizations. Although they live in fear of being discovered and ultimately reported, many eventually find success by blending into the community, finding work and living a normal life without catching anyone's notice.

In June 1993, a ship filled with undocumented Chinese immigrants ran aground off the coast of the Queens borough of New York City. The *Golden Venture* carried almost 300 refugees, who for six months had nearly circled the globe in

◀ Marine police officers in the town of Aberdeen, Hong Kong, apprehend men trying to immigrate illegally. A complex network of smugglers helps Chinese immigrants arrive in North America through routes that are often circuitous.

their small, rusty ship. At least 10 of the refugees died trying to swim to shore, while another 6 escaped into the United States undetected.

Eventually many of the refugees were deported back to China. In the following years, others who remained were granted political asylum. The *Golden Venture* incident brought the wretched conditions experienced by undocumented immigrants to the attention of the American media and fueled a public debate about refugees, political asylum, and human rights. Several similar incidents in which smugglers' boats have run aground along the coast of British Columbia have also taken place.

Snakeheads

Chinese smugglers of undocumented immigrants are often referred to as "snakeheads," since the often circuitous route of the smuggling operation to North America is like that of a snake. The "little snakeheads" get the Chinese immigrants out of China safely, sometimes by legal means but more often illegally. The "big snakeheads" bring the undocumented immigrants into the United States or Canada.

An undocumented immigrant typically perceives the big snakeheads to be business people instead of criminals. After all, the snakeheads are providing a needed service to Chinese immigrants, so it seldom concerns the undocumented immigrant that the smugglers are breaking U.S. or Canadian law.

Big snakeheads and their human cargo enter the country through a variety of routes and means of transportation. A few simply fly into North America from China, Hong Kong, or one of the southern Asian countries, but most travel on boats ranging in size from small commercial fishing boats to large transports.

Some Chinese undocumented immigrants sail to Central or South America and then come north by land through Mexico. There they join undocumented Mexican immigrants crossing the U.S.–Mexican border, usually in areas where human-smuggling operations are already well established. Once they reach the border, the immigrants will often have to wait several days or even weeks in a Mexican "safe house." When their guides decide it is safe to attempt a crossing, they are brought into the United States and transported to their final destination.

Some immigrants also cross over, rather more easily, from Canada to the United States, or vice versa. In *Human Smuggling*, published in 1997, Kenneth Yates describes how immigrants from the Fujian province would often fly into Canadian cities, then ask for political asylum in Canada or continue into the United States. Yates explains:

> Most aliens arriving [in Canada] from Fujian Province arrive at the Vancouver, Toronto, and Montreal airports.
>
> Current evidence indicates that a number of refugee claimants are delaying their entry into the customs inspection areas by hiding in bathroom facilities for several hours so investigators cannot ascertain which flight they arrived on. This is obviously an orchestrated ploy by the smuggling organizations to have the migrant evade detection.
>
> Once the aliens have been discovered in bathroom facilities, or after they enter the customs inspection area, they will immediately claim political asylum.

The air route is by far the most comfortable, consistent, and safest for immigrants coming illegally from China. It is, however, more expensive than the other routes and usually requires a forged passport and other documentation.

While it is cheaper, the sea route can be brutal for the undocumented immigrant. A 19-year-old who was smuggled to the United States from Changle, in Fujian province, told the story of her sea passage to researcher Ko-Lin Chin:

> We spent fifty-nine days on the mother ship. During those days, we ate twice daily. There was no water to wash ourselves, so we used seawater to brush our teeth and bathe. When we boarded the ship, every passenger was offered a thick paperboard and that was our bed. . . . When we were hungry, we tightened our belts. We did not even have the luxury to fill our stomachs with water when hungry. Many of us were seasick and could not eat much. Most of us lost a lot of weight, and we did not look like human beings.

Some passengers on the journey were denied water, developed skin diseases, or were assaulted by crew members.

Despite the hardships they may have endured in making their way to North America, some smuggled immigrants later become involved in the smuggling business themselves. For example, entrepreneurs from China's Fujian province have been known to form organizations, called *shetous*, whose members meet migrants at the point of entry, collect travel documents, and take the newcomers to safe houses. The undocumented immigrants are forced to remain in these facilities until they have fully paid for the smuggling operation. Smuggling fees can cost up to $30,000, of which the *shetou* receives 10 percent. *Shetous* are also responsible for processing applications and hiring attorneys to help those immigrants who are caught.

Paying Debts

Many undocumented Chinese immigrants can find work with Chinese employers, a fact that continues to draw immigrants to North America each year. Chinese owners of take-out restaurants often hire people from their own hometowns, and some arrive without proper documents. In the United States, most undocumented Chinese immigrants can apply for political asylum and are then allowed to work until their case is heard.

Smugglers may keep undocumented immigrants captive until their families or friends pay the smuggling fee. In some cases, the immigrants are kept in safe houses that are fairly sanitary, and they are provided with comfortable living conditions. But often residents are crowded into poorly heated, ramshackle dwellings or basements, where they receive substandard food and endure abominable conditions.

Those not held in safe houses must still pay off their debts. Sometimes they may be kidnapped and tortured, and relatives and friends who guaranteed payment may be threatened as well. In other cases undocumented immigrants are forced to pay off their debts by working for the smugglers or their associated gangs, sometimes as drug couriers, enforcers, or prostitutes.

Because they arrived in the country without legal documentation and fear for their deportation, they usually do not contact the police or other government authorities when mistreated or forced into jobs they don't want.

Tongs, Triads, and Gangs

Some of the smuggling of drugs and humans occurs through Chinese organized crime syndicates that have been reported to operate through tongs and triads (secret Chinese societies usually consisting of related members). Some American government officials have claimed that a significantly large share of money made from smuggling Chinese people goes directly into the tongs' pockets. In *Smuggled Chinese*, Ko-Lin Chin disagrees: "No doubt members of triads, tongs, and gangs are, to a certain extent, involved in trafficking Chinese, but I believe that their participation is neither sanctioned by nor even known to their respective organizations."

Most tongs are known to be involved in other criminal activities. These activites can entail the intimidation of those living in a tong-controlled territory of Chinatown. Tong members take

Chinese American teenagers who are prone to commit illegal activity may join gangs. These gangs, some of which have connections with the larger tong organizations of Chinatown neighborhoods, falsely promise power and influence to those youths who may lack employment and educational opportunities.

money from local businesspeople with the understanding that the association will keep other tongs from threatening the business. Some Chinese refer to this kind of bribe as "lucky money"—it makes sure that the tong doesn't do anything "unlucky" to the business, like smashing its windows or stealing its shipments of goods.

Some Chinese youth involved in criminal activity belong to Chinatown gangs, which may have tong connections. In New York City's Chinatown a tong-affiliated youth gang often enforces the tong's dictates on the streets. Some researchers have observed that immigrant teens may be drawn to gangs and later to tongs because through these groups they acquire power and influence in the community and are given important responsibilities. Others claim that many Chinatown gangs using the name *tong* actually have no connections to the larger associations. Instead the youth gangs are simply comprised of uneducated young immigrants dissatisfied with the lack of employment and economic opportunities.

In her book *Chinatown*, Gwen Kinkead quotes David Chen, executive director of the Chinese-American Planning Council, who sheds some light on how problems for Chinese youth have led to gang problems in some Chinatown neighborhoods. According to Chen,

> Many adults are illiterate in Chinatown. So the kids run the households. It contradicts the Chinese way of life, which is to respect the elders. It leads to a lot of problems: the kids hang out, there's not enough housing; there's not enough parental guidance; and at the same time, there's too much pressure for performance in school. They're all supposed to be stereotypical whiz kids. And those who aren't end up in gangs.

Racial Discrimination and Poverty

The Chinese in North America have endured a long history of discrimination. The 1882 Chinese Exclusion Act, which remained in place for 60 years, prevented immigration and naturalization on the basis of race. For decades the Chinese already living in the United States faced many obstacles: they were excluded from the right to obtain citizenship, vote, own land, or place their children in regular public schools.

The traditional Chinatowns used to offer a haven from physical danger for their inhabitants. Before the Second World War, Chinese children who ventured outside Chinatown in San Francisco, New York, or Los Angeles were frequently pelted with stones and garbage by white children. English-speaking natives would mock the Chinese language by making nonsense sounds. While the Chinese today generally face far less persecution and bigotry, it is still possible for ethnic tensions to develop.

Employment concerns can often impact how native residents feel toward new immigrants. When large numbers of foreigners settle in a neighborhood, its U.S.–born residents worry that their jobs will be taken by the newcomers. However, economic studies have shown this not to be the case. New immigrants not only benefit from coming to America, but their contribution to the economy also benefits their neighbors.

Today, the federal courts have become more active in defending the civil rights of Asian Americans than in years past, and the number of racially motivated crimes committed against Asian

A satirical cartoon entitled "A Statue for *Our* Harbor," printed in an 1881 issue of the San Francisco–based magazine *The Wasp*, represents the discriminatory attitudes that many Americans expressed toward the Chinese. The cartoon, which appeared a year before Congress passed the Chinese Exclusion Act of 1882, attributes a number of social problems, including immorality, disease, filth, and the ruin of "white labor," to Chinese immigrants.

Americans seems to have dropped off. In a summary of a study done in 2000, the National Asian Pacific American Legal Consortium (NAPALC) reported a 19 percent overall decrease in violent attacks against Asian Pacific Americans over the previous year.

The conditions found in Chinatowns during the 1960s reveal the extreme hardship and poverty endured by many Chinese who immigrated in those years. In his book *The Rice Room*, Ben Fong-Torres described the living environment typical of New York City's Chinatown at the time:

> Families of six to eight shared single hotel rooms, with a plank of plywood over a bathtub serving as a dining table. Clothes were stored in old trunks or stuffed into shopping bags hung on nails. Older single men slept in tiered bunkbeds in dank, closet-sized rooms.

During the 1960s many newcomers and residents suffered from malnutrition, lack of exercise, and tuberculosis. Similar problems existed in San Francisco's inner-city Chinatown. A 1970s study by researcher Ling-chi Wang recorded substandard housing in two-thirds of the living quarters, and tuberculosis rates that were six times the national average. However, conditions in these Chinese enclaves have improved markedly for immigrants, as the awareness of public health issues has grown.

China's Adopted Daughters

The Chinese government's implementation of the one-child policy, which is an an approach to resolving the overpopulation crisis, has had a significant effect on Chinese immigration. It has impelled many Chinese citizens who want to have more children to leave the country, and has also left many orphan girls available to be adopted by American parents. This second consequence is the result of the Chinese traditional culture's preference for males: sons remain a part of the family even after marriage, while daughters join their husbands' families. Some families have a daughter and can't obtain permission to have a second child, and so they decide to put the infant up for adoption in the hope that she will have a better life somewhere else.

An American eats at a Chinese restaurant with his newly adopted Chinese daughter. As a result of China's one-child policy, many Chinese families favor having sons, who will remain a permanent part of the family, and decide to put up their daughters for adoption.

Many American couples have adopted these infants. Since they are brought over from China as babies, most have no recollection of their mothers' or caregivers' faces or of the Chinese language or culture. Although some adoptive parents are Chinese, people of all ethnicities have also chosen to adopt Chinese girls. Non-Chinese adoptive families often face many decisions, including how to provide their daughters with information about the Chinese and Chinese American cultures and how to help them deal with prejudice or other issues they potentially face growing up in a different culture.

7 PART OF THE MOSAIC, PART OF THE MELTING POT

Asian Americans make up about 4 percent of the total U.S. population. Of the approximately 12 million people of Asian origin living in the United States, about 2.7 million of them are Chinese Americans, which makes them the largest Asian group in the nation. The Chinese living in Canada also form the largest Asian group, numbering more than 300,000.

A Growing Population

As the fourth-largest ethnic group currently immigrating to the United States, and the largest immigrant group entering Canada, the Chinese will continue in the years ahead to have a major impact on the face of North America. Although the Chinese and Chinese Americans made up only 1 percent of the U.S. population and 1 percent of the Canadian population in 2000, the continual stream of migration from China to North America will ensure that those percentages increase.

On average, each year about 40,000 legal Chinese immigrants enter the United States and over 30,000 enter Canada, according to the 2001 *Statistical Yearbook of the Immigration and Naturalization Service* and Canadian census figures. It is likely that the high rate of immigration from China to North America will continue. Although economic and political conditions in China have improved since the 1990s, convincing a

◀ The diverse populace of the United States is sometimes likened to a cultural mosaic, of which Chinese Americans—the largest Asian American group at an estimated 2.7 million people—make up a significant piece.

Ellis Island of the West

During the early 20th century, Chinese immigrants docking at San Francisco were quickly shuttled onto ferries that carried them to an immigration station located in the middle of the bay on Angel Island. From 1910 to 1940, this site was commonly referred to as the "Ellis Island of the West." Approximately one million immigrants, mostly from Asia, were processed at the facility.

But unlike Ellis Island, where most new immigrants usually waited a few hours for processing, Angel Island kept immigrants waiting for at least two to three weeks, and even as long as two years. They were housed in rough wooden barracks, kept under guard, and allowed out only for meals and to exercise in an area enclosed by a 12-foot-high barbed-wire fence.

The Chinese were kept in the Angel Island barracks for the longest period out of all the immigrant groups, because under the Chinese Exclusion Act of 1882 they were not allowed to enter the United States unless they were wives and children of American citizens or were entering as merchants, students, diplomats, or tourists. Before being approved to enter the United States, they were closely interrogated to determine their eligibility.

In 1970 a park ranger discovered Chinese calligraphy that had been carved into the walls of the barracks. It was in the form of poems written by immigrants living in the barracks. Eventually more than 100 poems were uncovered, most of them reflecting the fear and sadness felt by the Chinese forced to linger there. They have recently been documented by researchers as part of a $32-million eight-year project in coordination with the California State Parks and National Park Service to restore Angel Island and tell its story of early Asian immigration.

percentage of Chinese to remain where they are, the standard of living and high wages available in North America continue to attract tens of thousands of Chinese each year.

In the years ahead, immigration researchers will probably have difficulty charting the exact numbers of the Chinese immigrants illegally entering North America; however, some analysts believe that the steady flow of this immigrant group is unlikely to abate.

Making Significant Contributions

The influence of Chinese immigrants—both legal and undoc-umented—on Western society is apparent in the growing popularity of many aspects of their culture, particularly Chinese food, martial arts, and medicine. People of all ages

A white member of a kung fu athletic association leads a dragon dance in a Chinese New Year parade in Washington, D.C. Martial arts and other traditions preserved by Chinese Americans have made a significant impact on mainstream North American culture.

and ethnic backgrounds practice the Chinese martial arts of tai chi and kung fu, and ancient Chinese healing practices such as acupuncture and *qigong* have found a place in Western mainstream medicine.

Although they were prevented during the first half of the 20th century from obtaining citizenship and participating in political systems, Chinese Americans had begun making their presence known in politics and government by the 1970s. Through advocacy groups, they have worked to obtain and protect their rights in the United States and Canada. Today they serve in courtrooms, in city council chambers, in state-

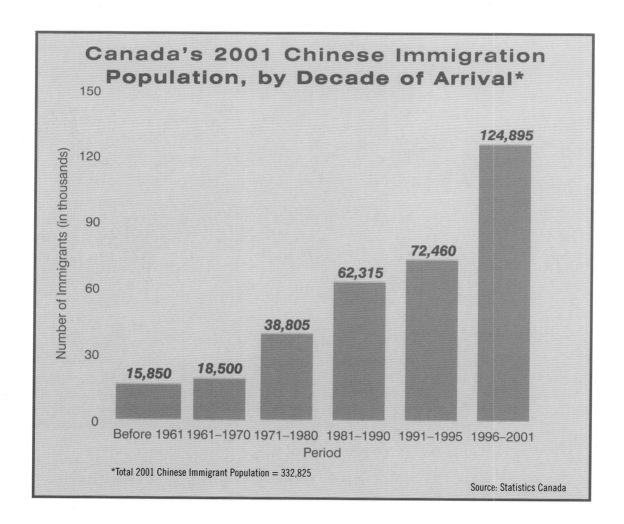

Canada's 2001 Chinese Immigration Population, by Decade of Arrival*

*Total 2001 Chinese Immigrant Population = 332,825

Source: Statistics Canada

houses and presidential offices, and in state, local, and federal government.

During the second half of the 20th century Chinese Americans continued to overcome hardships to make a place for themselves in the United States and Canada. Many Chinese Americans have been responsible for contributions in technology and science. They have helped design defense systems, silicon chips, computer software, and the Internet. Scientific researchers have received Nobel prizes for discoveries in chemistry and physics, and have developed treatments for deadly illnesses such as AIDS. Those living 100 or even 50 years ago could hardly have predicted the great impact that Chinese immigrants would make on American and Canadian life.

FAMOUS CHINESE AMERICANS/CANADIANS

Jackie Chan (1954–), Hollywood star, one of the few actors to perform all his own stunts; his action/comedy hit films include *Rumble in the Bronx* (1996), *Rush Hour* (1998), *Shanghai Noon* (2000), and *Shanghai Knights* (2003).

David Ho (1952–), chemist and director of the Aaron Diamond AIDS Research Center; his groundbreaking research work on protease inhibitors, which reduce the level of HIV, has helped allow AIDS patients to live longer after diagnosis.

Ji-li Jiang (1954–), children's book author; a former science teacher and founder of her own business, East West Exchange, she is the author of the award-winning novel *Red Scarf Girl* (1997), which is based on memories of her teenage years in Communist China. Her second book, *Magical Monkey King—Mischief in Heaven* (2002), is based on a Chinese folk tale.

Ang Lee (1954–), art-film director of *Sense And Sensibility* (1995), *Ride with the Devil* (1999), and *Crouching Tiger, Hidden Dragon* (2000), which won an Oscar for best foreign language film. Lee also directed *The Hulk* (2003), the blockbuster based on the comic-book hero.

Yuan T. Lee (1936–), chemist and recipient of the Nobel Prize in Chemistry in 1986 for his discoveries concerning the dynamics of elementary chemical processes; he was also awarded the National Medal of Science in 1986.

Bill Mow (1937–), founder, chairman, and CEO of Bugle Boy Industries, a casual-wear clothing line; he also holds a Ph.D. in electrical engineering.

I. M. Pei (1917–), architect, designer of modern skyscrapers, housing projects, museums, and academic and government buildings; for his designs he has received a multitude of awards, including the Medal of Freedom, Medal of Liberty, Grande Medaille d'Or, and Japanese Praemium Imperiale.

Vivienne Tam, fashion designer and founder of high fashion boutiques; in her book *China Chic*, published in 2000, she chronicled the history of Chinese dress and culture.

An Wang (1920–), founder of Wang Laboratories, a company that develops specialty electronic devices; his contributions to the development of digital computing machines helped revolutionize the information-processing industry.

FAMOUS CHINESE AMERICANS/CANADIANS

Wayne Wang (1949–), film director whose movies often deal with issues related to China and Chinese Americans; his most successful films include *The Joy Luck Club* (1993) and *Chinese Box* (1997), which is set before and during the transfer of Hong Kong from British to Chinese possession.

Harry Hongda Wu (1937–), geologist, writer, and activist; in 1985, after spending 19 years in a Chinese prison he immigrated to the United States, where he became an advocate for democracy and human rights in China.

GLOSSARY

assimilate—to become absorbed into a new culture.

asylee—a person who receives refugee status after arriving to a new country.

Cantonese—Chinese dialect originating in Guangzhou (also called Canton), southern China's largest city.

Communist—a follower of communism; a repressive political system in which most or all property is owned by the state and is intended to be equally distributed.

deportation—the forced removal of someone from a country, usually back to his or her native land.

enclave—a community that is culturally or ethnically different from its surrounding community.

eugenics—the controversial and disputed science of attempting to improve humans through breeding or through eliminating disfavored groups or characteristics.

green card—another name for an immigrant visa. It allows a legal immigrant to work legally, travel abroad, and become eligible for citizenship.

gross domestic product (GDP)—an economic indicator that measures the total value of domestic goods and services produced by a country within the course of a year.

homogeneous—having a uniform composition or structure.

Mandarin—the predominant dialect of China, spoken by over 70 percent of the population.

refugee—an alien outside the United States who is unable or unwilling to return to his or her country of nationality because of persecution or a well-founded fear of persecution.

tong—a Chinese association or club that is often associated with organized crime.

tongxianghui—a Chinese association of people who come from the same native place.

visa—official authorization that permits arrival at a port of entry but does not guarantee admission to the United States.

FURTHER READING

Boli, Zhang. *Escape from China: The Long Journey from Tiananmen to Freedom*. New York: Washington Square Press, 2002.

Chan, Anthony B. *Gold Mountain*. Vancouver, British Columbia: New Star Books, 1983.

Chang, Iris. *The Chinese in America*. New York: Viking, 2003.

Chen, Sucheng. *Asian Americans: An Interpretive History*. New York: Twayne Publishers, 1991.

Chin, Ko-Lin. *Smuggled Chinese: Clandestine Immigration to the United States*. Philadelphia: Temple University Press, 1999.

Evans, Karin. *The Lost Daughters of China*. New York: Tarcher/Putnam, 2000.

Fong-Torres, Ben. *The Rice Room: Growing Up Chinese-American from Number Two Son to Rock 'N' Roll.* New York: Hyperion Press, 1994.

Hutchings, Graham. *Modern China: A Guide to a Century of Change.* Cambridge, Mass.: Harvard University Press, 2001.

Jakobson, Linda. *A Million Truths: A Decade in China.* New York: M. Evans and Company, 1998.

Kinkead, Gwen. *Chinatown: A Portrait of a Closed Society.* New York: Harper Perennial, 1992.

Kuhn, Robert Lawrence. *Made in China: Voices from the New Revolution.* New York: TV Books, 2000.

Lee, Joann Faung Jean. *Asian American Experiences in the United States: Oral Histories of First to Fourth Generation Americans from China, the Philippines, Japan, India, the Pacific Islands, Vietnam, and Cambodia.* Jefferson, N.C.: McFarland & Company, 1991.

Miscevic, Dusanka, and Peter Kwong. *Chinese Americans: The Immigrant Experience*. Hong Kong: Hugh Lauter Levin Associates, 2000.

FURTHER READING

She, Colleen. *Teenage Refugees from China Speak Out.* New York: The Rosen Publishing Group, 1995.

Smith, Paul J., ed. *Human Smuggling: Chinese Migrant Trafficking and the Challenge to America's Immigrant Tradition*. Washington, D.C.: Center for Strategic and International Studies, 1997.

Takaki, Ronald. *Strangers from a Different Shore: A History of Asian Americans*. Boston: Back Bay Books, 1998.

Wong, William. *Yellow Journalist.* Philadelphia: Temple University Press, 2001.

Wu, Harry Hongda, and Carolyn Wakeman. *Bitter Winds: A Memoir of My Years in China's Gulag.* New York: John Wiley and Sons, 1994.

Zia, Helen. *Asian American Dreams.* New York: Farrar Straus & Giroux, 2000.

INTERNET RESOURCES

http://www.bcis.gov

The website of the Bureau of Citizenship and Immigration Services explains the various functions of the organization and provides specific information on immigration policy.

http://www.canadianhistory.ca/iv/main.html

This site contains an excellent history of immigration to Canada from the 1800s to the present.

http://www.c-c-c.org/

The Chinese Cultural Center of San Francisco has information about visiting hours, exhibits, and Chinese cultural events.

http://www.capa-news.org/

CAPA News is the main website for the Chinese American Political Association.

http://www.goldsea.com/

Gold Sea, an "Asian American supersite." This site deals with all sorts of news and events for Asians in North America and Asia.

http://www.ocanatl.org/

The national website of the Organization of Chinese Americans provides event listings, news, and activism information.

http://www.wn.com/s/chineseamericanews/

Chinese America News provides information on political and social issues pertaining to Chinese Americans.

http://www2.lib.ku.edu/eastasia/explore/china/chistory.htm

The University of Kansas East Asian Library presents information on Chinese immigration and provides links to other resources.

INDEX

Numbers in ***bold italic*** refer to captions.

INDEX

INDEX

SENATOR EDWARD M. KENNEDY has represented Massachusetts in the United States Senate for more than 40 years. Kennedy serves on the Senate Judiciary Committee, where he is the senior Democrat on the Immigration Subcommittee. He currently is the ranking member on the Health, Education, Labor and Pensions Committee in the Senate, and also serves on the Armed Services Committee, where he is a member of the Senate Arms Control Observer Group. He is also a member of the Congressional Friends of Ireland and a trustee of the John F. Kennedy Center for the Performing Arts in Washington, D.C.

Throughout his career, Kennedy has fought for issues that benefit the citizens of Massachusetts and the nation, including the effort to bring quality health care to every American, education reform, raising the minimum wage, defending the rights of workers and their families, strengthening the civil rights laws, assisting individuals with disabilities, fighting for cleaner water and cleaner air, and protecting and strengthening Social Security and Medicare for senior citizens.

Kennedy is the youngest of nine children of Joseph P. and Rose Fitzgerald Kennedy, and is a graduate of Harvard University and the University of Virginia Law School. His home is in Hyannis Port, Massachusetts, where he lives with his wife, Victoria Reggie Kennedy, and children, Curran and Caroline. He also has three grown children, Kara, Edward Jr., and Patrick, and four grandchildren.

Senior consulting editor STUART ANDERSON served as Executive Associate Commissioner for Policy and Planning and Counselor to the Commissioner at the Immigration and Naturalization Service from August 2001 until January 2003. He spent four and a half years on Capitol Hill on the Senate Immigration Subcommittee, first for Senator Spencer Abraham and then as Staff Director of the subcommittee for Senator Sam Brownback. Prior to that, he was Director of Trade and Immigration Studies at the Cato Institute in Washington, D.C., where he produced reports on the history of immigrants in the military and the role of immigrants in high technology. He currently serves as Executive Director of the National Foundation for American Policy, a nonpartisan public policy research organization focused on trade, immigration, and international relations. He has an M.A. from Georgetown University and a B.A. in Political Science from Drew University. His articles have appeared in such publications as the *Wall Street Journal*, *New York Times*, and *Los Angeles Times*.

MARIAN L. SMITH served as the senior historian of the U.S. Immigration and Naturalization Service (INS) from 1988 to 2003, and is currently the immigration and naturalization historian within the Department of Homeland Security in Washington, D.C. She studies, publishes, and speaks on the history of the immigration agency and is active in the management of official 20th-century immigration records.

PETER HAMMERSCHMIDT is the First Secretary (Financial and Military Affairs) for the Permanent Mission of Canada to the United Nations. Before taking this position, he was a ministerial speechwriter and policy specialist for the Department of National

CONTRIBUTORS

Defence in Ottawa. Prior to joining the public service, he served as the Publications Director for the Canadian Institute of Strategic Studies in Toronto. He has a B.A. (Honours) in Political Studies from Queen's University, and an MScEcon in Strategic Studies from the University of Wales, Aberystwyth. He currently lives in New York, where in his spare time he operates a freelance editing and writing service, Wordschmidt Communications.

Manuscript reviewer ESTHER OLAVARRIA serves as General Counsel to Senator Edward M. Kennedy, ranking Democrat on the U.S. Senate Judiciary Committee, Subcommittee on Immigration. She is Senator Kennedy's primary advisor on immigration, nationality, and refugee legislation and policies. Prior to her current job, she practiced immigration law in Miami, Florida, working at several nonprofit organizations. She cofounded the Florida Immigrant Advocacy Center and served as managing attorney, supervising the direct service work of the organization and assisting in the advocacy work. She also worked at Legal Services of Greater Miami, as the directing attorney of the American Immigration Lawyers Association Pro Bono Project, and at the Haitian Refugee Center, as a staff attorney. She clerked for a Florida state appellate court after graduating from the University of Florida Law School. She was born in Havana, Cuba, and raised in Florida.

Reviewer JANICE V. KAGUYUTAN is Senator Edward M. Kennedy's advisor on immigration, nationality, and refugee legislation and policies. Prior to working on Capitol Hill, Ms. Kaguyutan was a staff attorney at the NOW Legal Defense and Education Fund's Immigrant Women Program. Ms. Kaguyutan has written and trained extensively on the rights of immigrant victims of domestic violence, sexual assault, and human trafficking. Her previous work includes representing battered immigrant women in civil protection order, child support, divorce, and custody hearings, as well as representing immigrants before the Immigration and Naturalization Service on a variety of immigration matters.

MARISSA LINGEN is a freelance writer of educational materials. She lives in Hayward, California, and is working on a fantasy novel.

PICTURE CREDITS